PENGUINS

Past and Present, Here and There

King penguins on Macquarie Island.

PENGUINS

Past and Present, Here and There

George Gaylord Simpson

New Haven and London, Yale University Press

Library of Congress catalog card number: 75–27211
International standard book number: 0–300–01969–6
0–300–03095–9 (pbk.)

Designed by John O. C. McCrillis
and set in Baskerville type.
Printed in the United States of America by
Vail-Ballou Press, Inc., Binghamton, New York.

10   9   8   7   6   5   4   3

Contents

Illustrations

Preface

Penguins are habit forming. How I became addicted is briefly related toward the end of the first chapter of this book. I hope this book will lead others into this pleasant and generally harmless addiction. The Surgeon General has not determined that penguin watching is dangerous to your health, although I did once have reason to wonder about that. After years of penguin watching throughout the Southern Hemisphere, at many places with vile climates and hazardous approaches, I narrowly escaped death from pneumonia contracted while watching penguins on sunny islands at the equator.

Most penguin addicts have to obtain their fixes at zoos and in books. The author of one of the books is reminded of the classic remark by a small girl, that a book told her more than she really wanted to know about penguins. That gives a writer pause, and indeed Bernard Stonehouse, a great authority on living penguins, says that the girl's remarks put him off writing a book about penguins for nearly ten years. I have been involved with penguins for more than forty years, but it was my own insatiable curiosity (not only about penguins) and not the girl's remark that delayed my writing a book about them. This book is not for little girls, although they may read it if they wish. It is for adults who do not necessarily know much about penguins but for whom there is nothing that they do not really want to know. Obviously neither this nor any other book tells everything about penguins, or any other subject. I have tried to tell at least a little about most of the numerous and varied aspects of this extraordinary and entrancing group of birds.

Through the years I have become indebted to so many people for so many different kinds and acts of assistance in penguin

watching and studying that it would require another book to
name each individual and specify how he or she helped. I shall
just name the principal institutions in which I studied collections
of fossil or recent penguins and records or publications about
them: the American Museum of Natural History (New York),
the Museum of Comparative Zoology (Cambridge, Mass.), the
University of Arizona and the Simroe Foundation (Tucson, Arizona), the Museo Nacional de Ciencias Naturales "Bernardino
Rivadavia" (Buenos Aires), the Museo de La Plata (La Plata,
Argentina), the British Museum (Natural History) (London), the
Naturhistoriska Riksmuseum (Stockholm, Sweden), the South African Museum (Cape Town), the South Australian Museum and the
University of Adelaide (Adelaide), the National Museum of Victoria (Melbourne, Australia), the Otago Museum and the Univer-
sity of Otago (Dunedin, New Zealand), the Dominion Museum
(Wellington, New Zealand), the New Zealand Geological Survey
(Lower Hutt, New Zealand), and the Canterbury Museum (Christchurch, New Zealand). At several of these institutions staff members also took me penguin watching.

For information outside of my own observations, I have relied
almost entirely on the very extensive published literature, both
popular and technical, a small selection from which is listed at
the end of this volume. I must, however, mention that Dee Boersma,
Bernard Stonehouse, and Laurence M. Gould have assisted my
education about penguins in special ways.

The maps were drafted by Jay's Publisher's Services from rough
drawings by me. The figure of comparative sizes and the diagrams
of penguin heads with recognition patterns were drawn by Margaret
La Farge, also from my rough sketches. Figure 1 is from the New
York Zoological Society. Figures 2–4 are from U. S. Naval Sup-
port Antarctica RG 313 photographs in the National Archives
Building, Washington. Figure 9 is by Derek Green. Figure 11 is by
M. F. Soper; reproduction rights were granted by Bruce Coleman,
Inc. Figure 24 is a New York Zoological Society photo. The other
photographs are by me.

I am again indebted to my wife, Anne Roe, for encouragement and constructive suggestions.

I also thank the staff of Yale University Press, especially but not exclusively Anne Wilde and Catherine Iino, for assistance that goes beyond simple editing.

G. G. S.

Tucson, Arizona
November, 1975

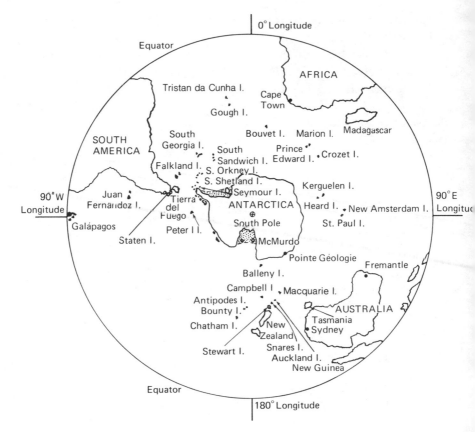

1. Sketch map of the southern hemisphere for orientation. Islands where penguins now breed are shown and named. Numerous other islands, especially in the South Pacific, are not shown. The projection of a hemisphere on a flat circle involves distortion, and the land areas are schematic only. The other maps in the text are drawn on the same base but omit most names. The stippled areas adjacent to Antarctica are the major ice shelves—Filchner upper left and Ross at the bottom.

1. Four Discoveries

There are eighteen living species of penguins. Unlike their stereotype, they are not confined to the Antarctic. Several extend into the tropics, and indeed one species lives right on the equator. The majority of them have long frequented coasts and islands that have also been frequented by humans for thousands of years. It would be absurd to think that those humans did not know that the penguins were there. Thus when we talk about "discovering" penguins we are using the word in a typically conceited, ethnocentric way. We do not think that anything has been discovered until a European has seen it, and even then we question the matter until the "discoverer" has returned home and written a book.

So it is with penguins. For thousands of years they were well known, but only by "natives," non-Europeans of Hottentot, Negroid, American Indian, Australian aborigine, and finally Polynesian stock (Map 1). Those people did not know how to write, and they long kept their knowledge to themselves. So as far as Europeans were concerned they never discovered anything.

In the European sense of the word, penguins were finally discovered twice. Although one discovery has clear priority, I am going to write about both. The discovery second in time was the first on public record, and it seems to me somewhat more interesting.

The first penguins seen by Europeans were undoubtedly the African species, those sometimes called blackfooted penguins, because indeed their feet are black (most penguins have pink feet), and sometimes "jackass" penguins, because even more than some of their South American relatives

1

sometimes given the same name they do indeed bray just like donkeys (no penguins have golden voices). Their scientific name is *Spheniscus demersus.*

That was the discovered species, but there is still some question as to the discoverer. The first European expedition to penetrate definitely into the range of those penguins was commanded by the Portuguese Bartholomeu Diaz de Novaes, usually known simply as Diaz or Dias. He had been an officer of the court of King John (João) II and he became vitally involved in the ambitious exploratory plans originated by Prince Henry, called The Navigator, although it was Diaz and the other seamen who navigated while Prince Henry stayed nearer home. (In fact Henry was dead before Diaz made his most important voyage.)

In 1487–88 Diaz rounded the tip of Africa and entered the Indian Ocean, thus proving that a sea passage to the East Indies was possible. He went up the east coast of Africa for some distance, but storms and tides prevented his striking out for India. After turning back, he discovered and named Cape Agulhas, which (and not the Cape of Good Hope) is the southernmost tip of Africa. He did also discover what we call the Cape of Good Hope after King John's "Cabo da Boa Esperança," but which Diaz called Cabo Tormentoso ("Stormy Cape"). Along that coast he should have seen penguins, but the records of his voyage are not extensive or firsthand and I have failed to find an undoubted mention of penguins in them.

Diaz received little credit for his great accomplishment, then or later. He did much to get Vasco da Gama's more publicized expedition under way, but he had no command in it and accompanied it only to the nearby Cape Verde Islands. It is ironic that he was later, in 1500, to drown in a storm off what he had prophetically called Cabo Tormentoso.

It was Vasco da Gama who gained the fame and awards

made possible by Diaz's discovery. After 1488, affairs in Lisbon were unsettled. It was nine years later and Emanuel I had succeeded to the throne before da Gama's flotilla set out on 9 July 1497. That voyage is well documented at firsthand, especially in what is known as the *Roteiro*, a Portuguese word meaning a descriptive itinerary. The original is lost; as it has come down to us in a contemporaneous copy, the *Roteiro* is anonymous, but it was first written by a participant in the expedition who served on the ship São Raphael under Vasco da Gama's brother Paulo da Gama.

On 22 November 1497 they rounded the Cape of Good Hope and went on first south and then east until on 25 November they came to a bay variously called São Braz, Sam Brás, or Sanbras, after the saint whose name in English is St. Blasius or St. Blaize. The point that bounds it on the south is still called Cape St. Blaize, but the bay is now called Mossel. It is at latitude 34°12′S, longitude 22°05′E, southwest of the town of George in Cape Province of the Republic of South Africa. The expedition remained there until December. The *Roteiro*, as translated by E. G. Ravenstein for the Hakluyt Society (the Portuguese version has not been available to me), remarks on the presence in the bay of an island on which seals of more than one kind were abundant and goes on to say:

> One day, when we approached the island for our amusement, we counted, among large and small ones [seals], three thousand, and we fired among them with our bombards from the sea. On the same island there are birds as big as ducks, but they cannot fly, because they have no feathers on their wings. These birds, of whom we killed as many as we chose, are called Fotylicayos, and they bray like asses.

The name Fotylicayos is a monstrous nonword, probably an error on the part of the scribe who made the surviving copy of the *Roteiro*. The Portuguese editor who finally published the book footnoted *Sotilicaires* as the correct name, but that has an appearance more French than Portuguese. A more recent Portuguese dictionary has the word *sotilicário*, which does indeed have a proper Portuguese sound and orthography. There is evidence that the name had previously been applied to northern birds, probably auks, which we will later find highly significant.

In any event the birds to which the author of the *Roteiro* referred as sotilicários, or something like that, were certainly penguins of the commonest African species, *Spheniscus demersus*. No other birds in that place could possibly have been described as flightless, seemingly without wing feathers (that is, not the plumage typical of most birds), and braying like asses.

Most students of such things now believe that da Gama's Angra de São Braz, our Mossel Bay, was Diaz's Golfo dos Vaqueiros ("Cowboys' Gulf"), and in any case it is likely that Diaz passed that way. Almost certainly there, and if not there then elsewhere along that coast, Diaz and his companions must have seen penguins and have become the first Europeans to do so. However, neither the voyage of Diaz nor those of da Gama (he went to India three times and died there) are known to have given that knowledge to the world. The *Roteiro*, the only document of those voyages known to have mentioned penguins unmistakably, was not published until 1838, by which time most of the living species of penguins were quite well known.

The effective discovery, the one that made the existence of penguins known to literate Europeans in general, was made at a somewhat later date in a different hemisphere, under a different navigator, and involving a different species.

The second European discovery of penguins was made on a voyage as famous as da Gama's, even more difficult and perilous, and to me, at least, even more interesting (Map 2).

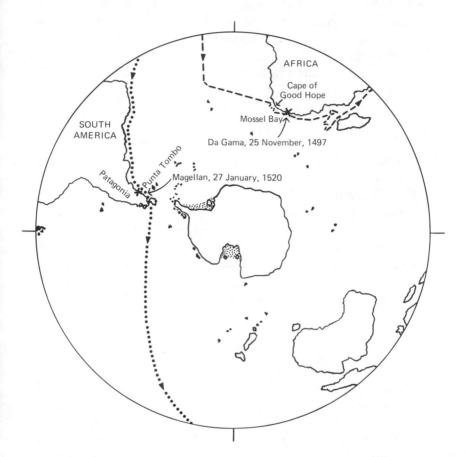

2. European discoveries of penguins. Approximate tracks of expeditions
first definitely known to have seen penguins: – – – – Vasco da Gama;
. . . . Magellan. Both expeditions also rounded South Africa from east to
west on their return, but those tracks do not involve discoveries in those
regions and are not shown. Points of discoveries of penguins are marked X.

That was the first circumnavigation of the globe, often referred to as Magellan's voyage around the world although in
fact Magellan himself did not make it around. He foolishly
became involved in petty local wars in the islands we now call
the Philippines and was killed there in a skirmish on 27
April 1521. There were and are no penguins in the Philippines
and the discovery had been made long before.

To go back a bit, Fernando Magalhães, whom we call
Ferdinand Magellan, was Portuguese by birth and served as
an officer under the Portuguese Crown. When the king of
Portugal refused him what amounted to a veteran's bonus, he
left in a huff, renounced his citizenship, and in 1517 became a
Spanish subject under King Carlos V. The Portuguese had
already found a way around Africa and eastward to the East
Indies and were making a good thing of it. Magellan readily
persuaded Carlos that the Spaniards could get in on the loot
by sailing *westward* to the Far East, around the tip of South
America. Five ships were fitted out, a company of unknown
exact size but on the order of 269 to 280 was recruited, and the
expedition set sail from Seville on 10 August 1519.

One of the most extraordinary things about that altogether
extraordinary expedition was that it included the first around-
the-world tourist, a gentleman who went along not as an
officer or other member of a ship's company but just for the
ride and to see what he could see. He was Antonio Pigafetta,
a native of Vicenza in Italy. In 1519 he accompanied the
papal ambassador to Spain, there learned of Magellan's im-
minent departure, and went along. He was wounded in the
same engagement in which Magellan was killed, but he
survived and unlike Magellan he did actually circle the globe.
On 8 September 1522 one of the original ships, the *Victoria*,
reached Seville with Pigafetta, the Captain (Sebastian del
Cano), and eighteen men. About an equal number of other

survivors straggled in later, but almost nine-tenths of the original company had dropped on the way from various causes, including pestilence, war, and capital punishment.

After his lucky return, Pigafetta soon went back to Italy, joined the Knights of Saint John (the Hospitallers), who had recently been driven out of Rhodes, and probably moved with them to their new home in Malta. The date and place of his death are not certainly known, but he probably died in Malta in 1534. The year of his birth is entirely unknown, but when he died he was at least in his sixties and possibly in his seventies, which was a ripe old age for that time and for one who had survived being shot by a poisoned arrow and other hazards of the first world tour.

Pigafetta set an example for later tourists: he kept a diary. If he had not, we would know little about the voyage. The few other available contemporaneous documents are much less complete or detailed. The original has not survived, and there has been much futile argument as to whether it was written in French or in Italian. There is no direct evidence that Pigafetta was literate in French, but he probably was. Most gentlemen of his station were. Nevertheless it does seem to me gratuitous to think that an Italian traveling with an ex-Portuguese navigator on a Spanish ship would have kept his journal in French. Pigafetta noted that he gave copies to Carlos V, to the Regent of France (mother of François or Francis I), and to the Grand Master of Rhodes (head of the Hospitallers, then Philippe de Villiers, of French origin), who was not in Rhodes at the time but in Italy. Those copies too, have disappeared.

There are four surviving manuscripts of Pigafetta's account that date from his period, although none is his original. One is in the Venetian 16th-century dialect of Italian and is in a library (Biblioteca Ambrosiana) in Milan. It clearly is not Pigafetta's original and had already undergone some rather inept editing. Two manuscripts in the French National Library in Paris are in 16th-century French. They differ from each other and the evidence is clear that they are independent translations from an Italian original, which was not the Milan manuscript. The other manuscript, now known as the Beinecke for its donor (Edwin J. Beinecke), is at Yale University. In 1969 the Yale University Press published a magnificent facsimile in color with a translation and annotation by R. A. Skelton. This manuscript, much the most elegant of the four survivors, is also in 16th-century French and also is clearly an independent translation from an unknown Italian original. It has been claimed that the Beinecke manuscript is the copy given by Pigafetta to the Grand Master of Rhodes, but its translator and editor, Dr. Skelton, considered this incorrect. The exceptional beauty and care of its rendition nevertheless indicate that it was made for some important and doubtless wealthy personage.

It was not in fact any of these or of earlier now lost manuscripts that gave news of the discovery of penguins to the European world in general. That was done by a slightly more abbreviated version of Pigafetta's account printed in Paris for a bookseller named Simon de Collines. The volume was not dated and some recent students date it in 1525, while others think it was issued after 1526 and perhaps as late as 1536. In any event it was printed while Pigafetta was still alive. It again is in 16th-century French and again, like the surviving Paris manuscripts, it represents an independent translation from a lost Italian original.

In passing, it is interesting that Shakespeare, who cribbed so much raw material and transmuted it into gold, lifted some details of *The Tempest* from Pigafetta's narrative. One of these details is the name Setebos for a supposed Patagonian god or demon. For some reason this was omitted from the Patagonian vocabulary in the first printed version, but it does occur in the narrative part of that text, and other texts were also available by the time Shakespeare wrote *The Tempest* (1611). It is included in the vocabulary given in the Beinecke and other manuscripts.

On such a voyage at such a time the tourist could not fail to see many strange and wonderful things. That Pigafetta did. He may occasionally have exaggerated a bit, but he was not like those medieval travelers who reported things not merely wonderful but downright impossible, a fault of which even the nonpareil Marco Polo was sometimes guilty. What Pigafetta reported he had in fact seen. That is our real business with him here, for among the things he saw were penguins, new and strange because equation with those encountered in Africa during da Gama's voyage was not made at the time.

Admirers of the quaint may like to have the announcement of the discovery in 16th-century French. I have transcribed this from the facsimile of the Beinecke manuscript. The version published by Simon de Collines is essentially similar but somewhat curtailed; for example, it speaks only of *ouoyes* and not of *oyes* and *oysons*.

> De deux isles plemes [pleines]
> de oyes doysons et
> loups marms [marins]

Depuis en enfuyuant le mesme chemin/vers le pol antartique/allant la coste de terre/nous trouuasmes deux isles pleines oyees [oyes] et oysons/et loups marins Dont on ne scauroit extimer la grande quantite quil y auoit de ces oysons: Car nous en chargeasmes tous les cinq nauires en vne heure/Lesquelz oysons sont noirs/et ont les plumes par tout les corps dune mesme grandeur et facon/et ne volent point/et viuent de poisson. Et estoyet si gras quon ne les plumoit point/mais on les escorchoit/et ont le bec comme vng corbeau.

The passage is translated by Skelton as follows:

> Of two islands full of geese, goslings,
> and sea wolves

> Then following the same course toward the Antarctic
> Pole, coasting along the land, we discovered two islands
> full of geese and goslings and sea wolves. The great
> number of these goslings there were cannot be estimated,
> for we loaded all the ships [the French text has "all five
> ships," G.G.S.] with them in an hour. And these goslings
> are black and have feathers over their whole body of
> the same size and fashion, and they do not fly, and
> they live on fish. And they were so fat that we did not
> pluck them but skinned them, and they have a beak like
> a crow's.

Although "sea wolves" is the literal translation of the
French original, the animals in question were certainly seals.
In a note to his translation Skelton assumes that they were
fur seals, which is possible, but it is much more likely that they
were sea lions. Both would have been called sea wolves by
Pigafetta, and both are called simply wolves (*lobos* in Spanish)
by Argentinians to this day.

The "geese" and "goslings" were certainly penguins. The
facts that they do not fly (in the air, that is) and live on fish
are indicative, as is the fact that they are so fat that they need
to be skinned, obviously to prepare them as food. The com-
ment that they have similar feathers throughout refers to the
absence of flight feathers or pinions, a peculiarity that early
struck all observers of penguins and still does. That is clearer
in the Beinecke manuscript than in the Simon de Collines
publication, which says that "elles nont pas plumes." That
would normally be read "they do not have feathers," meaning
that they have no real feathers at all, suggestive of the *Roteiro*
statement that the African penguins "have no feathers on

their wings." The translator of Pigafetta into French, who
certainly had never seen a penguin himself, would have made
the matter clearer if he had written 'elles nont pas pennes,"
that is, "they have no pinions."

There is a possible but not serious catch. The Simon de
Collines publication says that the "ouoyes . . . sont noires par
tout," ("the geese are black all over") and the Beinecke
manuscript says that the "oysons sont noirs" ("the goslings
are black"). No penguins are black all over, and the penguins
seen by Pigafetta, certainly the species we now call *Spheniscus
magellanicus*, are not absolutely black but are dark, usually a
slaty or even bluish gray, on the back, much of the head, and
most of the outer side of the wings, although, as in all penguins,
the breast is light. We can, however, take it that Pigafetta
meant only that the general color is dark, and it is also noteworthy that in juveniles, which are specified in the Beinecke
manuscript, the dark coloration is somewhat deeper and more
extensive than in adults.

Penguins do not at all resemble geese. It is incredible that
Pigafetta really considered them to be a sort of geese, and it
is thus mysterious that he called them geese. He certainly did,
as this occurs in all versions of his account. I can only infer
that having encountered birds so completely outside his
experience and vocabulary, he used "geese" as a sort of non-
descript term for birds in general, not as a particular term for
relatives of *Anser*. An idle etymologist might find amusement
in investigating this possible usage.

The place where this discovery was made is of special con-
cern. It has often been assumed that this was in the Strait of
Magellan. The late Robert Cushman Murphy, a great
authority on penguins, thought it was in the Gulf of San
Matías on the Patagonian coast of Argentina. Skelton, a
great authority on Pigafetta, thought it was off the mouth of
the Río Deseado, also in Patagonia. I believe that those and

all other previous suggestions were wrong and that the locality can be much more probably determined.

The problem arises mainly because Pigafetta was vague, indicating only that the discovery was made after they left what is now identifiable as the Río de la Plata and before they reached what is now identified as San Julián, where they went into winter quarters. That in itself rules out the straits, not entered until after they left San Julián, but it leaves the whole Argentine coast north of San Julián open to question. There are sources other than Pigafetta, and among them most notable is a *Derrotero* (Spanish equivalent of the Portuguese *Roteiro*) by one Francisco Albo (or Alvo, which is pronounced the same in Spanish). The original is said to be in Simancas, Spain, but the version available to me is from a copy made by Juan Bautista Muñoz in 1783 and now in the British Museum. It consists largely of "altitudes of the sun" and derived latitudes taken daily when weather permitted, but some observations on events and on lands seen are included.

Albo's latitudes, where they can be rechecked, are surprisingly accurate for that epoch and those conditions. For example he gave the latitude of San Julián as 49⅔° south. (Pigafetta, who was probably being tutored in navigation by Magellan and later wrote a treatise on the subject, gave it as 49½°.) That place is exactly identifiable and still has the name given by Magellan. Modern maps give its latitude as 49°17'S, so Albo was only 23 minutes off. (Pigafetta was even closer.) Albo does not mention penguins, but on 27 January 1520, before they reached San Julián, he found the latitude to be 44°S, with a bay to starboard (west) and two rocks (islands), and further along on the same day there was another bay with many seals ("lobos de mar"). It was just in this part of the voyage that Pigafetta mentioned two islands with many seals, along with penguins. Around 44°S on the Patagonia coast there are several small bays, still frequented by seals and penguins and with various small outlying rocks. This is, indeed, almost exactly the latitude of Punta Tombo (44°5'S) near which there is a large penguin rookery evidently of considerable antiquity. It is a good guess, or rather more than a guess, that Pigafetta's notice that gave the news of penguins to the European world referred to 27 January 1520 and to this part of the coast.

Albo's *Derrotero* is specific that the expedition left the Gulf of San Matías (which Magellan named) two days earlier, that is on 25 January. He gave the latitude there as 42½°, which is only about 20 seconds off for the southern edge of the gulf. This was before and north of the penguin discovery and rules out the Gulf of San Matías as the locality. There is no evidence in the *Derrotero* or elsewhere that Magellan's party identified the Río Deseado, but its mouth is at latitude 47°44'S, hence more than three and a half degrees south of what seems clearly to be Albo's latitude for the penguin discovery. Nowhere was Albo so mistaken in a latitude, and I believe that this rules out the mouth of the Deseado as the locality.

Between the author of the *Roteiro* and Antonio Pigafetta the European discovery of penguins had been well and truly made, although one thought they were auks and the other called them a strange kind of geese. Much more is to be said about what they truly were and are. First, though, let us continue with discovery and consider that penguins, like all other living things, have long, long histories. One way of studying such histories, not always the most conclusive, is by fossil remains of ancestors and relatives. The next two finds for discussion in this chapter are of fossil penguins. The first of them takes us to an island whose existence was not even imagined in the days of da Gama and Magellan. The second will take us back to the part of the world where Pigafetta first saw living penguins.

So far as there is any record, the first fossil penguin ever discovered was found in New Zealand. The record is indeed scanty, to such an extent that no one bothered to write down the name of the actual discoverer. The place concerned is on the east coast of the southern part of the South Island (southwestern of the two main islands) of New Zealand. Here centered on the market town of Oamaru there is a prosperous region devoted to sheep raising, like so much of New Zealand, but also to cattle, to a variety of grains, and to some industry. About five miles south of Oamaru along the coast is the village of Kakanui. Those are native Maori names and *kakanui* in Maori refers to a kind of not especially choice fern root. Oamaru has no recorded meaning except as a place name, but there may be some connection with the fact that one of many meanings of *maru* is for a soft, fissile stone.

However that may be, from early European settlement in that area toward the middle of the 19th century, beds of soft limestone were quarried for building blocks. This grew into an extensive industry and still continues but now on a reduced scale and mostly for interior facing because much of the stone is too porous and soft to weather well. The material has usually gone by the generic name of Oamaru Stone, but sometimes also Kakanui or earlier Kakaunui Stone. Several different beds of stone are involved. It was in one of those beds at Kakanui probably in 1858 or early 1859 that a curious bone was found. It was not stated but can be surmised that the discovery was incidental to early quarrying of stone or lime for local use; commercial exploitation is said to have started about 1860. The discoverer was a "native," that is, a Maori, and the reason why his name was not recorded can also be surmised. That unsung discoverer took the fossil to the local savant, a Dr. W. B. D. Mantell, who forwarded it to a world authority on such things and many others: Thomas Henry Huxley. With it Dr. Mantell also sent notes on the local geology. In order to bother the great man with this, Mantell must have had an inkling of its importance, especially as he had himself published papers on fossil moas, extinct birds of New Zealand, but that is something else we do not know. Huxley merely acknowledged that "Mr. Mantell" had sent him the specimen and some geological notes.

Huxley recognized the find for what it was: the first known fossil penguin bone. He published an excellent description and two woodcuts of it in 1859 in the *Quarterly Journal* of the Geological Society of London. The specimen is still preserved in the British Museum (Natural History) in Cromwell Road, London, which is one of the Meccas for students of penguins. It is the peculiar bone of birds that represents a fusion of what were in the reptilian ancestors of birds separate ankle bones and metatarsals—the bones that form the arch in our own feet. This compound, fused bone is absolutely typical in penguins, unmistakable once seen, and it also is diagnostic of each of the different kinds of penguins.

The bone sent to Huxley is larger than in any living penguin and differs in other less obvious ways. He saw that it could not belong to a living species or genus and so correctly gave it a new name: *Palaeeudyptes antarcticus* Huxley, 1859. That could be freely translated as "the ancient skillful diver from the Antarctic," and it incidentally, amusingly, reveals a bit of provincialism on Huxley's part. London, where Huxley wrote and chose this name, is much nearer to the North Pole than Kakanui is to the South Pole.

Since 1859 many more bones of fossil penguins have been found in New Zealand. Even there the record leaves much to be desired, but it is richer and more nearly continuous than for any other region. There will be more to say about it later. Perhaps, however, I should make just one more remark at this point. I have mentioned that Huxley's (or the anonymous Maori's) fossil indicated a penguin larger than any now living.

It did *not* indicate one of the purely mythical penguins six or seven feet tall that have found their way into many popularizations and even into at least one technical work. As nearly as can be judged from the scanty material *Palaeeudyptes* can hardly have exceeded 4 feet 9 inches in height, and the largest known extinct penguin was probably well under 5 feet 4 inches.

Fossil penguins were discovered in Australia about 1888, but for a long time were not recognized as such, and the first published notice of them did not appear until 1957. Some were found on Seymour Island, near the coast of Antarctica, in 1903 and first described in 1905. The first fossil penguin was not found in South Africa until 1970, published in 1971. Although I will include all those finds in later general discussion of fossil penguins, narratives of each discovery need not be given here. (Interested historians can find them through citations in the appendix to this book.) Fossil penguins were discovered in South America not long before 1891 and first published in that year. For a special reason immediately to become obvious, I do intend here to discuss not so much *the* discovery as *a* discovery on that continent.

All fossil penguins known from South America to this day are from Patagonia, an informal name for the southern part of the Argentine mainland. *Patagón* in Spanish means big foot, so this is, or rather was, the land of the big feet, a name given by Magellan and recorded by Pigafetta. Pigafetta noted that the people of this land were "giants" and also that they wrapped their feet in skins, which made them seem even disproportionately large. They would not have seemed gigantic or particularly big-footed to us, but the Spanish explorers, certainly lacking nothing in toughness, were small men with dainty feet. Now Pigafetta's "giants" are long gone, as such, although they still have descendants most of whom speak a dialect of Spanish and consider themselves inheritors of European blood and culture.

The fossil penguins found in their land, so near to where Pigafetta found living penguins, are varied as to species but are all of the same geological age. All so far known are from rocks deposited as sediment by a sea advancing about 35 million years ago over what had before been land and is now land again. Almost all of these relics have been found in just two regions, one around the settlement of San Julián in latitude 49°17'S and the other around the town of Trelew, considerably farther north in latitude 43°13'S. This brings Pigafetta to mind again, because he first saw penguins not far from the present site of Trelew, and with Magellan and the rest of the expedition he spent five months in the harbor of San Julián over the southern winter of 1520. One would like to think that Pigafetta whiled away the time picking up fossil penguin bones, and he may perhaps have seen some, but he did not mention them in his diary. Magellan, in any case a man more of action than of letters, was there occupied with a mutiny, which he quelled quite effectively by executing two of three ringleaders and marooning another there "with a priest," as Pigafetta laconically says. Later brief records (not in Pigafetta's account) suggest that there may have been two marooned priests, that they were implicated in the mutiny, and that the marooned group did not perish there but was rescued by Gómez, who abandoned Magellan in the strait and turned back.

An annotation of Pigafetta has caused some geographic confusion by assuming that San Julián was the same as the place later called Puerto Deseado, or Port Desire in English. Both are ports in the present Province of Santa Cruz, but they are separate places about 130 miles apart as the crow (or should it be the condor?) flies. Fossil penguins have not been found at Puerto Deseado.

Trelew, the principal center for fossil penguins in South America and not far from a principal area for living ones as well, is a true oasis in bleak Patagonia. It is on the Chubut

River, one of the few important watercourses of Patagonia, fed by streams from the distant Andes. The valley is narrow, but irrigation and the efforts especially of a band of Welsh immigrants who fled from the English to this remote spot have made it blossom. The town of Trelew is one of the more important places in Patagonia and even when I first visited it in 1931 it had such un-Patagonian facilities as a hotel, a bank, a school, and reasonably well-stocked stores.

The climate of Patagonia is one of the worst on earth, and it has not changed since Pigafetta's day or earlier. In the 1930s there had been changes in other aspects of Patagonia, but outside of a few centers, Trelew high among them, it was still fascinatingly savage. Now, alas! like almost every place on earth it has become overrun and dully tame.

When I visited Trelew in 1931 my party was on its way back to Buenos Aires after a highly successful season of collecting fossils farther south. We did not take the time to look for fossils around Trelew, but in 1933 I was back there to begin another collecting campaign. Coleman Williams, "Coley," a North American who had been with me on the previous trip, was again on this one, and in Trelew we were joined by Justino Hernández, a Patagonian lad (now, like me, a happy grandfather), the extremely good outcome of the extraordinary marriage of an Araucanian Indian to a Lithuanian woman. Justino also had been in our earlier party. We were accompanied more briefly by Alejandro Bordas, who at that time was connected with the national museum in Buenos Aires.

After a difficult trip from Buenos Aires, which we had left on 17 October, we finally reached Trelew on 7 November and two days later began the field work for which we had come so far and with so much difficulty. My speciality was, and still is, fossil mammals, warm-blooded, milk-giving like ourselves, and it was their remains that we sought. Of course we were also quite willing to pick up anything else if we ran across it and it seemed really to have scientific importance. Like Pigafetta I keep diaries of my even more extensive but less world-shaking travels, and I have just now been rereading the entries for that November back in 1933. (November is of course spring down there.) I am surprised to see how little stress I placed on our discoveries of fossil penguins. As the mystery writers used to say, "Had I but known!"

Here is the diary entry including my first direct encounter with fossil penguins:

> San Teodoro. Thursday, November 9. This morning Poppe ran us out to the barranca opposite Gaiman and literally ran us over the barranca, for he leaps like a mountain goat. We got some orientation for later use there. Lunch at Dean's school, amongst all the infants. Later with young Dean, Poppe, and two young Poppes to Cerro Castillo, opposite here, also for orientation. Found shark teeth and penguin bones enough to warrant a few days' work. We thought of stopping at the nearest house, but a very stern Señora said "No. I have daughters, and you know what will happen to them if I take these men"—Coley and me—"into the house." We hardly knew whether to feel flattered or not. At any rate, no hospitality awaited us there lest we rape the damsels, so we arranged with a boliche near the river to stay with them.

Some points require a gloss for wider comprehension. The saint's name is from an Argentine calendar with a saint for each day of the year. I took to entering them in my diary because that amused me; the Patagonian climate can engender a bizarre and childish sense of humor. Herr Poppe, a most cooperative friend, was manager of the local branch of a German trading company. He provided transportation because our own, after the brutal overland trip from Buenos Aires, was out of commission. Gaiman is a smaller, originally also Welsh settlement, a short distance up the Chubut Valley from Trelew. A barranca in Patagonia is a cliff or large, steep slope. (Usage of the word is somewhat different in southwestern United States.) The Cerro Castillo, "Castle Peak," is a steep-sided erosional remnant of sedimentary rock in the desert just south of the valley. Not only our first but also most of our later fossil penguins came from there. A boliche is a sort of combination country bar-café-store-inn, which sounds rather grand, but in the 1930s, at least, the Patagonian boliches were all of a primitiveness and crudity that in retrospect seems incredible. Nevertheless we stayed in them when available near our work because that saved the time and manpower of setting up and maintaining a camp. In this situation, given the state of the roads and trails and of our transport, the hotel in Trelew was too far away and also more expensive.

We stayed in the Trelew–Gaiman area until 24 November 1933 and did make quite a good collection of fossil mammals of an ancient fauna hitherto barely known. Also as what we thought was quite incidental, we made the largest single collection of fossil penguin bones that had ever been made or, indeed, has been to this day.

Back at the American Museum of Natural History in New York City, where I was at that time Associate Curator of Fossil Mammals, I sorted out the penguin bones and offered them for study to a number of ornithologists. Those who were studying fossil birds begged off because they were too busy studying other and different kinds of birds. Those who were particularly interested in penguins studied their skins (not preserved in any fossils), did not know how to identify their bones, and did not care to learn. So the splendid collection lay around for some time while I happily studied Patagonian fossil mammals and unhappily spent a couple of years in the army. Back in New York in 1944 I determined that if no one else would study the fossil penguins, I would do it myself. I did so and gave the results in a monograph published by the Museum in 1946. Without relinquishing my primary interest in mammals, I have been studying fossil penguins off and on ever since and have now examined all those known from anywhere. This has naturally also stimulated my interest in living penguins, and I have now visited most of the existing species on their native heaths—or ice floes.

Thus, initially almost by accident, I have inherited a tradition that stems from the unknown author of the *Roteiro*, from Antonio Pigafetta, from Thomas Henry Huxley, and from many others, and I am carrying it on in this book about the past and present of some of the most curious and fascinating creatures on earth.

2. Naming Penguins

This chapter is about how penguins, severally and singly, received their names. The beginning will seem irrelevant, but as lawyers are supposed to say in the big trial scenes, "I will connect it up."

Early on 4 June 1844 three Icelanders, Sigurdur Islefsson, Ketil Kentilsson, and Jon Brandsson, set out to hunt geirfugl. Until 1830 geirfugl had been common enough on the relatively large island called Geirfuglasker for that reason. In 1830, however, a volcanic eruption completely wiped out the population on that island. A few geirfugl did survive on nearby smaller islands, and the three hunters had heard that there were some on Eldey. The price had gone up as the prey became scarce, and an offer of one hundred crowns apiece was worth considerable effort and some danger.

Kentilsson had no luck, but Islefsson and Brandsson succeeded in killing the last two geirfugl on earth.

Fugl in the Norse name means bird, but the original meaning of *geir* in this compound is unknown. From geirfugl the English early adopted the mispronunciation "garefowl." Another Norse name for them was *alka* (the Swedish form), and from that the English made "auk." The garefowl specifically was the largest of the auks and so was called the "great auk." Another name for it was "penguin."

The origin of that name is obscure, to say the least. A popular idea, still to be found in some dictionaries, is that penguin is the Welsh *pen gwyn*, which means white head. The trouble is that the Welsh people had little to do with these birds and especially that the garefowl, the original penguins, happen to have black heads. Even more far-fetched, indeed ridiculous guesses would derive the name from Latin *pinguis*, (fat), or from English "pin wing."

Wherever it came from, the name penguin was applied to the great auk or garefowl from an early date. In his compilation of voyages Hakluyt quoted a letter from Parkhurst dated 13 November 1578 about a voyage to Newfoundland. Among other things Parkhurst wrote that in that region, "There are many other kinds of birds store, too long to write, especially at one Island called Penguin where we may drive them on a planke into our ship as many as shall lode her. These birdes are also called Penguins and cannot flie." There is some evidence that they were being called penguins by sailors long before Parkhurst wrote. Parkhurst's "Island called Penguin" has been identified. It is now called Funk Island and lies off the coast of Newfoundland in latitude 49°46′N, longitude 53°13′W, some 80 miles northeast of Gander. Much of what we know about these birds comes from skeletons and natural mummies found there.

Obviously these birds were not what we now call penguins. They belonged to a completely different order and were related to the little auks and to the guillemots, some of which have survived and which can fly. Technically they were called *Alca impennis*, now often changed to *Pinguinus impennis*. Well within historic time they were widespread and lived in great numbers around the North Atlantic. They bred along more northerly cool shores, although not into the Arctic, and in winter spread as far south as the Bay of Biscay in Europe and Cape Cod, or rarely even to northern Florida, on the American side. They could not run, climb, or fly, and if cut off from the sea they were easy prey. Their meat if not good (recorded opinions differ) was at least edible, and all agreed that their eggs were savory. Skins and fat also had uses. Even so the American birds survived for more than two centuries after their discovery. They were probably all gone by about 1800.

The extinction of the species on 4 June 1844 was dastardly, but it was only the last act in a decline already irreversible. The whole has often been cited as an example of man's inhumanity to his fellow creatures, but the facts of life and death are not so simple. Recall, for one thing, that the last fatal decline in numbers off Iceland was not by the hand of man but by what has been legally called an act of God: a volcanic eruption. Garefowl had been common in association with man for thousands of years before they gradually disappeared. They had been abundant in Greenland when first sighted but soon vanished completely there with no clear evidence of unduly extensive slaughter or so-called overkill, although that has been claimed.

There is also a possibly relevant parallel. Neither garefowl nor penguins (in the present sense of the word) have ever occurred in the North Pacific, but there was there a family of birds (called Mancallidae) that were adaptively similar, flying underwater but not in air. They became extinct before man had evolved and we cannot be blamed for their passing. It is at least possible that the extremely specialized garefowl had evolved into a dead end and were bound for extinction, the usual end of species in general. We cannot condone the act of Islefsson and Brandsson, but they only put a date on the inevitable course of nature.

There is no doubt that the name penguin was first applied to the northern garefowl or great auk and only later transferred to the southern birds. That causes no confusion now because the name is no longer used in any but the latter sense. It bothers only historians and readers of old travel tales, who are confused by references to penguins in places like Newfoundland, and perhaps also readers of a classic:

Ile au Pingouins (*Penguin Island*), by Anatole France. However, that should not be too troublesome for that book (first published in 1907) is not really about penguins of either kind. It is a satire, both funny and bitter, on the French army, the Catholic church, the bourgeoisie, and numerous other things not admired by the author. In its opening passages a holy man is miraculously wafted to an island inhabited by "penguins." Being short-sighted and hard of hearing, he takes them for humans and baptizes the lot. That raises a dreadful problem in heaven, but the theological issue is solved by the Lord's transforming the birds into men, who can legitimately be baptized and become good Christians. Thereafter they act just as stupidly as original humans, and the whole book becomes a cynical version of the history of France—the country, not the author.

It is clear that Anatole France's "penguins" were intended to be great auks and not what we call penguins, but annotators and publishers have assumed the opposite. Recent illustrated editions of the book show the holy father, Saint Maël, blessing a mob of adélie penguins, an Antarctic species.

It is clear enough how the transfer of the name by early travelers occurred and has become standard. Pioneers are rarely profound etymologists or zoologists. When they encounter a new animal or bird they often call it by the name of some perhaps only vaguely similar creature they knew back home. An example is familiar to everyone: when the English settled in North America they called one of our birds a robin, because it has a red breast like one in England. Yet the two are quite different, *Turdus migratorius* in America, *Erithacus rubecula* in England.

There was no European name for the southern birds now called penguins. They had native names, of course, and Pigafetta may have recorded one. In the Beinecke manuscript, discussed in Chapter 1, Pigafetta gives a list of words in the Patagonian Indian language ("Vocables des Geans Pathagoniens"). Here is included "A goose: Chache" ("Vne oye/Chache"). As Pigafetta called penguins strange geese, it is at least possible that he considered "chache" (which would be pronounced *shahsh*) the Patagonian name of what we now call penguins. Pigafetta's calling the southern penguins strange geese seems rather far off the mark, but Pigafetta, an Italian who had hitherto traveled only in Spain, certainly had never seen and probably never heard of a garefowl or northern penguin. Anyone who had seen one would almost certainly have noticed the resemblance between those and the southern birds and have transferred the name from one to the other. In fact if *solilicário* was indeed a Portuguese name for the great auk, the author of the *Roteiro* had already done that even before Pigafetta's time.

The great auk, original penguin, was a heavy black and white bird, breeding on shore and seeking its food in the sea. It had lost the power of aerial flight but used its still powerful wings to swim, in fact to fly, in the water. It did not swim with its feet as so many waterbirds do. In all these respects and in general appearance it was quite like the southern birds to which one of its names became attached.

Transfer of the name penguin to the southern birds was surely done by a sailor, and probably an English sailor, who knew the northern birds of that name. There has been some confusion as to just when that transfer became current, but some contemporary records, mostly published by Hakluyt, pin it down fairly well.

In 1578 Francis Drake followed Magellan's path along the coast of Patagonia. Like Magellan he spent most of a winter at San Julián, where Magellan's gibbet was still standing, and like Magellan he there found reason to execute a member of his crew; the Patagonian climate is trying even in summer and awful in winter. Drake's man at least suffered a more gentlemanly fate: he was not hanged but beheaded. Later that winter, on 24 August 1578 (August is late winter in those latitudes) Drake "arrived at an Island in the streights [of Magellan], where we found great store of foule which could not flie, of the bignesse of geese, where we killed in less than one day 3000. and victualed ourselves thoroughly therewith." The "foule" were of course penguins, but nowhere in relations of Drake's voyage do I find them called by that name.

Another account, by John Winter, who sailed with Drake, makes it clear that Drake named three adjacent islands in the "streight," the largest Elizabeth, next Bartholomew, and smallest St. Georges. The slaughter of penguins was on St. Georges, which is now called Santa Magdalena. It is at 52°50'S, 70°40'W, about 25 miles northeast of Punta Arenas.

Winter's description of the penguins is worth quoting, even though it antedates their naming as penguins:

> Here we staied one day & victualled our selves with a kinde of foule which is plentiful in that isle, and whose flesh is not farre unlike a fat goose in England: they have no wings, but short pineons which serve their turne in swimming. Their colour is somewhat blacke mixt with white spots under their belly, and about their necke. They walke so upright, that a farre off man would take them to be little children. If a man aproch any thing neere them, they run into holes in the ground (which be not very deepe) whereof the island is full. So that to take them we had staves with hookes fast to the ends, wherewith some of our men pulled them out and others being ready with cudgels did knocke them on the head, for they bite so cruellie with their crooked bils, that none of us was able to handle them alive.

(Who was acting "cruellie"?)

Francis Petty's account of Thomas Candish's (or Caven-
dish's) voyage around the world in 1586–88 has the earliest
application of the name penguin to the southern birds known
to me, although there may be earlier. On 17 December 1586
the expedition entered a Patagonian harbor (in Petty's spelling
"harborough") which was named Port Desire after Candish's
flagship, *The Desire.* That locality, at 47°44′S, 65°56′W, still
has the name given by Candish, but now translated into
Puerto Deseado. I doubt whether any present resident knows
the origin of the name; none did when I was there.

Petty remarked that there were islands with seals and birds
just off Port Desire and his first description of the birds,
although it did not name them, made it clear that they were
penguins. Later he wrote that on 28 December they left Port
Desire and went on to an island "where we trimmed our
saved pengwins with salt for victual." There is no evidence
as to why he suddenly started calling them penguins (in his
more phonetic spelling). Later he tells us that on 8 January
1587 they were at "Pengwin Ilande" in the "streights of
Magellan" where they "killed and salted great store of
Pengwins for victuals." Another account of the same voyage,
by Thomas Fuller, makes it clear that their "Penguin Island"
(variously spelled) was the islet named St. Georges by Drake.
(It has been erroneously supposed that Drake called it
"Penguin.")

John Jane wrote an account of a later voyage by Candish,
starting in 1591. Candish himself died on the voyage in 1592
and the pitifully few survivors reached Great Britain at last
in 1593. In that account Jane speaks of "Penguin-isle" near
Port Desire and then of "an Island in the Streights called
Penguin-isle." This duplicate nomenclature, which was used
by English navigators, at least, for some time, has confused
historians. The two islands are far apart, by nearly 400 miles
in a straight line, and in different modern countries, Argentina

and Chile. The one near Port Desire, now Puerto Deseado, is still called Isla Pingüino. As previously noted, the other was Drake's St. Georges and is now Santa Magdalena.

Thus before the end of the 16th century the southern birds were generally called penguins in English, and that usage eventually spread to all other learned languages.

In France the great 18th-century naturalist Buffon became exercised by British stupidity in giving the same name to the northern birds, then not yet extinct, and to the similar but zoologically quite distinct southern birds. He proposed to confine the old name to auks and razorbills and to call the southern birds *manchots*, meaning one-handed or one-armed in French and thus applied by Buffon because of the supposed loss of function of the wings. As (southern) penguins in fact have two wings, both completely and strongly functional, this was not a happy example of French clarity and logic. Nevertheless Buffon's authority was such that the name caught on for a time in France and is still sometimes used in this sense, although now rarely.

Use of "penguin" or its derivatives as the popular or vernacular name for the southern birds, only, has now become practically universal in literary languages, including Spanish *(pingüino)* and French *(pingouin)*. It is, for example, *pingüim* in Portuguese, *pinguino* in Italian, *pinguin* in German, the equivalent of *pingvin* in Russian, the equivalent of *pengkouin* in modern Greek, and so on.

So much for the name penguin and how it came to be transferred to its present usage. I previously mentioned in passing that there are eighteen species of living penguins. (There is a slight difference of opinion about that, to be considered later.) These live in different areas and have different characteristics and habits. There is no such thing as *the* penguin, and to be lucid and significant we must distinguish one from another. Although all are penguins in the broad sense, each kind (species) must therefore have its own particular name. There are two distinct systems for naming birds and most other animals, both in simultaneous and about equal use. That seems redundant and indeed rather silly, but we shall have to use both here for the otherwise poor reason that everyone does.

One system is that of so-called common or popular or vernacular names. Sometimes these are indeed the names long used by the common people who live where the birds (or other creatures) are and who know them at first hand and not from books. Such names are real and useful; they are part of a natural language. Much more often, however, the "common" names are made up by the writers of books and are quite unknown to the local people until, for example, a visiting ornithologist tells them that what they have always called a *kororaa* is "really" a "little blue penguin" because the books say so. Nevertheless there is something in favor of calling it a little blue penguin, because many people find that easier to remember and to say than kororaa, which is a Maori word.

The same might be said in favor of "little blue penguin" as opposed to *Eudyptula minor*, which is the name of the same species in the other current system of nomenclature, the scientific taxonomic system. Some people think the scientific system is too difficult, but they overemphasize the difficulty and underestimate the advantages. Parents are often surprised at how readily children pick up scientific names (of dinosaurs, for example), and even if we admit that the children are probably brighter, parents are not necessarily that stupid. *Hippopotamus* does not really bother parents, yet it is a scientific name and a hard one, five syllables and like so many scientific names a latinized concoction from Greek roots. One of the hippopotamus's really vernacular or common names is *kiboko* in Swahili.

One of the great advantages of the technical system is that common names are often ambiguous while scientific names are precise and distinctive. It was mentioned before that the common name "robin" designates two quite different birds, whose scientific names, *Turdus migratorius* and *Erithacus rubecula*, make confusion impossible. There are examples also among penguins. Both the most frequent South African and the most frequent Patagonian penguins are commonly called jackass penguins, but they are different species, *Spheniscus demersus* in South Africa and *Spheniscus magellanicus* in Patagonia. Moreover, in scientific nomenclature each of those species has just one name and no doubt about it. Each has more than one common name: blackfooted or jackass penguin for the first; magellanic or jackass penguin for the second (not to mention some older Spanish and native names still occasionally encountered, such as *pájaro niño*, *pájaro manco*, or *burro*).

The scientific system has another advantage: it indicates in part, although not in complete detail, the similarities and relationships among the organisms named. Thus both the South African and the Patagonian penguins have the first (generic) name *Spheniscus*, indicating that although they are different species they are quite closely related. The different first name of the New Zealand *Eudyptula minor* indicates more distant relationship. Still more broadly the system of nomenclature has been developed from one formalized by the 18th-century Carolus Linnaeus, a Swedish botanist who also classified and named animals. It depends on a hierarchy or sequence of categories, each smaller than the last, something like nested boxes. Thus a class is a large group that includes smaller orders, which include still smaller families, and so on down. Applied to our subject and carried as far as we need for present purposes and in a form modified from that of Linnaeus, the classification and nomenclature go as follows:

Class Aves (all the birds)
  Order Spherisciformes (all the penguins)
    Family Spheniscidae (still all the penguins; the
        Spherisciformes include only one family although
        some orders of birds include many families)
      Genus *Spheniscus* (and five other genera in the
          family Spheniscidae)
        Species *Spheniscus magellanicus* (and three
            other species in the genus *Spheniscus*, plus
            fifteen species in other genera of Spheniscidae)

The scientific names accepted as valid are the first ones given in published works. They are adopted or made up by their authors and put in Latin or at least pseudo-Latin form. Commonly they are in fact of Latin origin, also frequently from Greek transliterated into Latin, but they can be from any language or name. The name of a species is always two words; the first is capitalized and is the name of the genus to which the species belongs. The second, specific name is not capitalized and is commonly an adjective or the possessive of a person's name (but respectable scientists do not name species after themselves). Both names should be printed in italics.

The name of a family is made by combining a part (the stem) of the name of an included genus with the suffix *-idae*. *Spheniscus* is the type genus of the family Spheniscidae to which all known penguins, fossil and recent, belong. That seems especially appropriate as *Spheniscus* included the first penguins to be seen by Europeans, both in Africa and in America, but there is no rule that the first genus found or named is also to be the family type. To many readers *Spheniscus* may not seem an appropriate type for the whole penguin family, because this genus does not include the stereotype penguin, the absurd little gentleman in a dress suit. That penguin, as we will see in due course, is named *Pygoscelis adeliae* and is quite distinct from any species of *Spheniscus*.

It has rather lately become customary for students of birds, but not other animals, to name orders by adding -*iformes* to the stem of the name of a typical genus. The order of penguins was long known as Impennes, which is neo-Latin for "feather-less" and perpetuated the early impression that penguin feathers are not really feathers. With *Spheniscus* generally accepted as typical of the group, the order is now universally known as Sphenisciformes.

Some people with peculiarly orderly or, I would say, rigid minds have been bothered by the fact that the content of the Order Sphenisciformes and the Family Spheniscidae are exactly the same, although in general an order in classification is defined as a higher or more inclusive category than a family. This has even been given a name, "Gregg's paradox" (although John R. Gregg did not perpetrate it; he was just among the first to complain about it), and a rather precious esoteric literature has grown up around it. In my opinion, which is not universal, the situation is really very simple. The height of a category indicates not only and indeed not neces-sarily how inclusive it is, that is, how many groups of lower categories it contains. Its height also indicates how different its members are from the members of other categories. As we shall see, penguins differ among themselves, but they differ no more than do members of other families of birds. There-fore it is reasonable to put them all in one family. But as we shall also see, they differ enormously from any other family of birds. It would be absurd to indicate in classification that their distinction is only that of one family from another. It is at least as great as that of one order, a higher category, from another. Therefore they logically and reasonably constitute not only a family of their own but also an order apart.

All the known extinct penguins also belong to this same family and order. It would have been possible for some branch to become distinctive enough to be put in a separate, related family, but no evidence of that is in hand. The very remote earliest members of the order must primordially have emerged from some different primitive ancestral order, but the incomplete fossil record so far recovered does not carry us back that far.

Within the family, the extinct members are named on the same system of genera and species as are recent penguins and other animals. For them, however, there is no system of common names. Personally I hope no one ever bothers to devise one, although I am so inconsistent that I do regularly use both common and scientific names for all the living penguins.

What's in a name? What does a name mean? There are two quite different answers, and it is important to distinguish them. One is the meaning inherent in the origins of the words used as names. These are not necessarily significant or even properly applicable to the things named. My name, George Simpson, is derived from words meaning "a farmer whose father was named Simon," but I have never been a farmer and my father's name was Joseph. In fact "George Simpson" means a certain person, me, and has nothing directly to do with farmers or their fathers' names. So, too, *Spheniscus magellanicus* means a particular species of penguins and for that meaning the origins of the words are irrelevant.

Nevertheless there is something to be derived from the origins of names of birds and other organisms. We will later meet the various genera and species of living penguins as such, but in the meantime their names can afford us some entertainment and indeed some food for thought.

The generic name *Aptenodytes* is derived from Greek roots meaning "featherless diver." "Diver" is appropriate enough. "Featherless" is not, but we have already seen that the peculiar, distinctive structure of penguin feathers made some observers believe that they are not really feathers.

Aptenodytes forsteri was named in honor of Johann Reinhold Forster (1729–98), a naturalist on Captain James Cook's voyage around the world and one of the earliest scientific describers of penguins. His son Johann Georg Adam Forster (1754–94) served as his assistant on that voyage. The popular name of these penguins is "emperors," a fitting but not very imaginative recognition of the fact that they are the largest living penguins.

Aptenodytes patagonicus is a misnomer in that there seems to be no evidence that these penguins ever lived in Patagonia, strictly speaking, but they have occurred as close as Tierra del Fuego and the Falkland Islands and "Patagonia" was construed rather broadly by early narrators. The popular name is "king penguins," because they resemble emperor penguins but are somewhat smaller.

Megadyptes, a generic name, is Greek for "big diver." There are three penguins larger than these, but they are larger than the average.

Megadyptes antipodes is the only species of this genus. It was so named because it lives in what, if you are British, is part of the antipodes, southern New Zealand and smaller islands still farther south from there. The popular name is yellow-eyed penguin, and it is indeed yellow-eyed, but why not call it by its excellent Maori name *hoiho*? (See remark on *Eudyptula minor* at the end of this list.)

The generic name *Pygoscelis* is from Greek roots with the rather odd meaning "rump-legged." It is true that when penguins stand erect their legs seem to issue from their rumps, and I suppose that is the idea of the name. (Come to think of it, we humans are pygoscelid, too!)

Pygoscelis adeliae means "Adélie's pygoscelis." This is the stereotype penguin, the little man in evening dress, the best known of all penguins both popularly and scientifically, and it is pleasant that both its scientific and almost identical popular names have a rather romantic derivation. Their godmother was Adélie Dumont d'Urville, the wife of the

French explorer and naval officer Jules Sébastian César Dumont d'Urville (1790–1842). Among his many exploits was command of the *Zélée* in southern seas in 1837–40. I have not seen a picture of Madame Dumont d'Urville, but I am sure that she was beautiful. Her husband surely had an eye for beauty, for it was he who saw to it that the Venus de Milo was saved and transported to the Louvre. The popular form of the name for this species is "adélie penguins."

Pygoscelis antarctica is obvious enough and appropriate, for indeed only the adélies and the emperors range farther south than these. The popular name, "chinstrap," is also fairly obvious, for this species is distinguished by a thin black straplike line under the chin.

Pygoscelis papua was so named by the Forster of *Aptenodytes forsteri*, but this was a howling blunder on his part. He named these penguins for Papua, a Malay name formerly applied to all of New Guinea (now only to a part of it), under the impression that the same species occurs in New Guinea. There are no penguins in New Guinea and almost certainly never have been. What's in a name, indeed? Although this name is obviously wrong in its implication, it cannot be changed under the International Code of Zoological Nomenclature. The usual popular name for these penguins is "gentoo," but there is something wrong with that, too. The name was first applied to this species by English-speaking people in the Falkland Islands, but in English usage a gentoo is an inhabitant (usually pagan or Telegu) of India. In fact no one knows how this peculiar application of the name to penguins came about. The sealers used to call these penguins johnnies, which is less outré but also of unknown origin and now abandoned in favor of the bizarre name gentoo. (I have never seen this suggestion elsewhere, but it occurs to me to wonder whether the white band over the head, present in no other penguins, suggested a turban to the Falkland Islanders.)

The name *Eudyptes* is Greek for "good diver," quite apropos, although equally so for any genus of penguins. With six species, this is the largest genus of living penguins.

Eudyptes chrysolophus is the macaroni penguin. *Chrysolophus* means "golden crested," in reference to the plume of bright yellow feathers on each side of the head, present in all species of *Eudyptes* but perhaps most striking in this one for its richer, almost orange color. The popular name "macaroni" has an interesting origin that relates also but indirectly to American colonial and revolutionary days. The name does indeed derive from the Italian pasta macaroni, but it has come a long way from that. In the 18th century there was a Macaroni Club in London whose members were fops with foreign ways such as eating outlandish Italian foods. They also adopted affected styles including a "Macaroni coiffure," which seems to have resembled the more recent teenage affectation of the ducktail hair style. The crests of *Eudyptes chrysolophus* recalled to sailors the silly Macaroni hairdo. And early Americana? One version of *Yankee Doodle* has the line "Stuck a feather in his cap and called it Macaroni." This otherwise seeming nonsense is simply a putdown for the ridiculous airs of the English with their London Macaronis and other dudes.

Eudyptes schlegeli was named for one H. Schlegel who was publishing on birds in the Netherlands around the middle of the 19th century. The penguin, another with yellow crests, was presumably given the common name "royal" because it is handsome, although in my opinion no more so than several other species. Or perhaps there is some reference to the fact that on its main breeding ground (Macquarie Island) it is associated with king penguins.

The penguins popularly called erect-crested have sometimes been technically called *Eudyptes atratus* and sometimes *Eudyptes sclateri*. The problem arose because the name *atratus* was based on an abnormal specimen that could have belonged to

either of two different species. The name *sclateri* is not ambiguous and is being officially adopted for this species. Philip
L. Sclater and his son William L. Sclater (1863–1944) were
both British ornithologists and I am not sure which was the
godfather of this species, but I think the latter. The popular
name erect-crested fits well because in all other *Eudyptes*
penguins the crests hang down behind and in this they bristle
upward.

Eudyptes crestatus is a nondistinctive name because all *Eudyptes* are crested (*crestatus* in Latin or pseudo-Latin). In fact
the classical Latin would be *cristatus,* but J. F. Miller, who
gave this name in 1784, wrote "*crestata.*" Under the Code
we can correct his error in gender (*Eudyptes* is masculine so
crestatus has to be also), but we cannot correct his *e,* which is
probably wrong but may be a Latin variant not in my
dictionaries. The common name is "rockhopper," which is
both picturesque and apt. These penguins commonly have
their rookeries in steep, rugged, rocky places where they hop
about with an agility extraordinary in birds so seemingly
clumsy on land.

The specific name of *Eudyptes pachyrhynchus* means "thick-
billed" and the bill is stouter than in most penguins of other
genera but less so than in some other species of *Eudyptes.* Its
popular name, "fiordland penguin," refers to its occurrence
in the fiordland of New Zealand, on the west coast of the
South Island.

Eudyptes robustus is indeed somewhat larger and thick-billed,
in those senses more robust, than its closest geographic and
zoological neighbor *E. pachyrhynchus,* but it is not otherwise
particularly distinctive. Its popular name, "Snares Island
penguin," refers to its locality. It apparently breeds only on
that one small island south of New Zealand, but it does
forage more widely and occasionally lands on other shores.

The generic name *Spheniscus,* which as we have seen also

provides the root for names of the whole penguin family and order, is latinized Greek for "little wedge." Everyone seems to agree that this refers to the shape of the wings, but they do not look like little wedges to me.

Spheniscus magellanicus is named for the Straits of Magellan, where, as we have seen, this species does occur. It is not named directly for Magellan; if it were, its name would be *Spheniscus magellani*. The common name now usual is "magellanic penguin." It has also often been called "jackass penguin" because it brays, but all species of *Spheniscus* bray, and the name is more frequently applied to *Spheniscus demersus*, a champion brayer.

Spheniscus humboldti was named after Friedrich Heinrich Alexander von Humboldt (1769–1859), whose travels in Latin America in 1799–1804 and his later attempt to describe everything in the universe (*Kosmos*) made him famous. The popular name "Humboldt penguin" is sometimes given, but "Peruvian penguin" is more usual. Its range is indeed mostly Peruvian.

Spheniscus demersus is the African penguin. *Demersus* means "plunged" in Latin, which is not very distinctive for a penguin. Nor is "jackass," often used as a popular name, very distinctive for a species of *Spheniscus*. "Blackfooted penguin," the more usual and perhaps less derogatory name, is also not clearly distinctive in this genus. I do not know why this species is not simply called the African penguin.

The Galápagos penguin, so called as a popular name, is *Spheniscus mendiculus*. *Mendiculus* is Latin for "little beggar." This is one of the smallest penguins—only the next two species are smaller—and "beggar" may apply to the babies' quest for food from their parents, but all baby penguins do that.

Eudyptula, the final generic name, derives from "good little diver." Like all penguins, these do dive well, and they are the smallest.

Some authorities do not recognize *Eudyptula albosignata* as a species fully distinct from *Eudyptula minor*, a point for later consideration. *Albosignata* derives from "white-marked," which refers to white on the wings, and the popular name is "white-flippered penguin."

Eudyptula minor is, as its specific name implies, the smallest living species. It is usually called "little blue penguin." It is not in fact blue but has a pale, slaty, perhaps vaguely bluish back, contrasting with the darker backs of most other penguins. Its Maori name is *kororaa* and, as Maori is still a living language, it seems a pity that this distinctive, really vernacular name has not been adopted instead of a synthetic "popular" name.

3. The Basic Penguin

Pygoscelis adeliae has probably figured in more cartoons than any other creature except *Homo sapiens*. A cartoon figuring both of those species has as a setting the mouth of a cave far up a precipitous mountain. Seated before the cave is a bearded, robed, turbanned *Homo sapiens*. He is faced by an adélie penguin, *Pygoscelis adeliae*, who is asking, "Why can't penguins fly?" The guru's answer is not given, but a student of penguins can readily give at least four answers, one now considered wrong, the other three, each in its own way, all correct.

The wrong answer is that penguins can't fly because their lineage branched off from that of other birds before flight had evolved and they neither inherited nor developed that faculty. This view was never held by a majority of students, but for a time (last in the 1930s) it was seriously argued on scientific grounds by a small minority. There is now no real doubt that all animals classified as birds had ancestors that were aerial flyers and that those lacking aerial flight, now quite a few and formerly even more numerous, have lost that ability.

The first right answer is purely mechanical and takes the weights of penguins and the sizes of their wings as given. Birds have complex mechanical requirements for flight, varying greatly with their different sizes and different ways of flying. Consider, for example, a tiny hummingbird, wings in constant motion so rapid as to be practically invisible to the human eye, able to hover or to move in any direction, even straight backward, and compare a large frigate bird, able to soar for hours without flapping its wings, always moving forward in relation to the air around it. Obviously other factors are involved as well, but a mechanical feature important for all birds is that of wing loading, which is the ratio of weight to the area of the wings. Wing loading varies considerably and is generally but irregularly less for small than for large birds. In other words, small birds tend to have larger wing areas in proportion to their weight.

There is what may be called an architectural reason for that. If one bird has a body twice as long as another's, it will probably be about eight times as heavy. But if its wings are also twice as long, their area will tend to be only about four times as large. The wing loading therefore would be about twice as great, the ratio being eight to four. To keep the wing loading the same, the wings would have to be not twice but nearly three times as long (more exactly 2.83 times, as an average tendency). This discrepancy increases greatly with increase in size. For example, a frigate bird may weigh up to 3,000 times as much as a hummingbird. In order to maintain the same wing loading, the frigate bird would have to have wings about fifty times as long as the hummingbird's. The frigate bird's wings are indeed much larger, but not that much; in fact, although the figure is variable it is usually less than forty.

Even though large, heavy birds can in various ways get by with high wing loadings, up to about five pounds per square foot (about 2½ grams per square centimeter), there is a definite limit beyond which aerial flight becomes mechanically impossible. Penguins cannot fly (in the air) because their ratio of weight to wing area is far beyond the mechanical limit of wing load for any aerial flier.

Why do penguins have what offhand may seem to be such a disadvantage? That leads to the second correct answer to the adélie's question to the guru. This answer is that in the course of their evolution there came a time when it was advantageous to them to increase the weight–wing ratio beyond the point of possibility for aerial flight. This apparent loss was not a loss from the point of view of survival and it was favored by natural selection. That is true of all flightless birds, but for different reasons in different groups.

Flight serves numerous functions, but especially food seeking, evasion of predators, and migration. If all of these functions become useless to a group of birds, flight will tend to be lost just because there is then no natural selection favoring it, and useless functions tend to become reduced or lost in the absence of stabilizing selection. That was evidently true in such instances as the flightless Galápagos cormorant. Wings were of no help in obtaining its food, as it swims only with its feet. Predation was slight when it evolved; there were no land predators on the islands. The equatorial climate and year-round fish supply made migration unnecessary.

In other instances special circumstances gave greater selective value to characteristics incompatible with aerial flight. For the big running birds—ostriches, rheas, emus, and cassowaries—the advantages were increase in bulk well beyond that possible for an aerial flyer and evolution of exceptionally rapid ground locomotion impossible for smaller birds. (A ridiculous sight my wife and I once saw was an emu running with a mob of full-out large kangaroos and keeping up with them at about 40 miles an hour.)

The penguins also lost aerial flight because it was incompatible with a different, accessible, and highly successful way of life. In that way of life they always seek their food and, except while rearing young or molting, spend most of their lives at sea. Many aerial fliers do the same, yet they did not occupy a whole series of ecological niches left open for occupation by ancestral penguins. These involve larger, bulkier birds able to pursue animal food actively under water.

The third correct answer to "Why can't penguins fly?"

issues directly from the first two. It is this: in fact penguins
can fly. Most birds fly in the air. Many of them swim in the
water, paddling with (usually) webbed feet. Penguins do
neither. They fly in the water. They do have webbed feet
but they use them as rudders and not for propulsion. They are
propelled in the water by their wings, which move in unison
as in usual flight and are as heavily muscled as those of
aerial fliers. The breastbones of penguins have high keels for
muscle attachment as in the aerial fliers. Ostriches and other
flightless running birds have greatly reduced wing muscles
and unkeeled almost flat breastbones.

Some of the details of the evolutionary transition from aerial
to aquatic flight will be considered later. So will particular
variations and adaptations to special ecological situations
among the different species. Here we are concerned with
their adaptive characteristics in a broader sense, those common
to all penguins and making them penguins, birds so peculiar
as hardly to seem to be birds. An obvious place to start has
been just in this matter of flight, and some further consideration should be given to its most obvious instrument, the wing
or flipper.

The penguin wing is tapered, pointed, and flat. It is somewhat flexible, but in striking distinction from wings of aerial
fliers it has practically no free motion at the joints except
where the upper bone (the humerus) meets the shoulder
girdle. It may seem anomalous that a penguin wing looks
rather more like that of a fixed-wing airplane than do most
birds' wings. The leading edge is rounded and the following
edge tapers off, reducing drag and increasing propulsion.
The reduction of feathers both on the wings and over most of
the body to small, scalelike things that so puzzled the early
discoverers also reduces drag without losing considerable
capacity for insulation. Without pinions, the wing is long,

narrow, and pointed, capable of strong propelling action in a medium so much denser than air.

That shape also gives the wing a smaller area relative to its length than in most aerial birds. Together with the relatively large, stout, heavy body the narrowness of the wing further increases the wing load, but wing loading is not an essential limitation for penguins. In the air, wing action, whether active as in flapping or passive as in soaring, must keep the whole body suspended against the pull of gravity as well as propelling it. When a penguin is in water its weight is essentially canceled out and the wings need do little more than propel it forward. That entails another peculiar specialization of the basic penguin.

If penguins were much lighter than water they would have a sort of wing-loading problem in reverse. It would require considerable wing power and muscular activity not to keep them up but to keep them down as they pursued their food below the surface. Aerial birds have had the weight to be lifted decreased by the evolution of light bones and of air sacs, some of them even within the bones. In penguins the buoyancy to be overcome has been decreased by just the opposite evolutionary trend. They have no air sacs except for the lungs essential for respiration, and their bones are solid and dense. They generally thus weigh just a little less than the amount of water they displace and so require little energy either to remain submerged or to stay on the surface.

The whole penguin body is effectively streamlined, ideally suited to their peculiar method of propulsion in the water. They have another strange behavioral trait when they are not feeding but are just traveling in the sea. They frequently swim under water until they get up a good speed then shoot upward and forward into the air for some distance before they drop back into the water and start renewing their speed.

While in the air they coast; they have no means of propulsion in that element. The rapid repetition of this sequence is called "porpoising," and while everyone who has ever seen penguins at sea has noticed it, the explanations I have seen are not entirely convincing.

Unlike most seals and whales, penguins cannot or at least normally do not stay under water for more than a few minutes at a time, in fact no longer than is possible for an experienced human diver without apparatus. When they emerge they breathe rapidly to restore oxygen, then breathe out, not in, before submerging again. Obviously when they are porpoising they breathe during the jump, or glide, and it has been supposed that that is the reason for this mode of travel. However, it would seem simpler for them just to stick their heads out of water and keep on swimming, as they do when they are not in a hurry to get somewhere. This is pure conjecture, but it seems to me that porpoising may decrease the effort and increase the efficiency of their longer, more rapid trips. They readily gain speed by wing action in the denser medium, but if they stop using their wings the drag there, even on their streamlined bodies, would rapidly use up their momentum. If they periodically go up into the air, the much lesser drag permits them to move along for some distance with no further propulsion and no great loss of momentum. However that may be, the sight of a group of penguins porpoising along—one wants to say "gaily," but of course we don't know what their emotions are—that sight is at first incredible, always exciting and unforgettable.

Penguin locomotion on land may seem even more peculiar to human observers than their locomotion in the water. They are more at home in the water, but much time must be spent on land or, in cases that are exceptional and not the rule as sometimes supposed, on ice. The eggs must be incubated on land (or ice) and it is some time after hatching before the young can feed themselves. They are at first covered with fluff that would waterlog them if they went into the water where their only food is, and until they acquire the slick, more adult plumage they have to be fed by their parents. Fully molting adults have the same problem and have to go without food until a new coat is acquired.

Penguin locomotion, both in the water and on shore, ties together in a functional way that is quite unbirdlike. In aerial birds the tail is almost always a necessary part of the total airfoil. When such birds land, the body plus tail is in more nearly horizontal than upright position and the fore-and-aft center of gravity is above the feet. If these aerial birds also swim, they usually do so with the body, considerably lighter than water, floating high and the feet acting as paddles more or less below the middle of the body. In penguins the tail may serve as a stubby prop when they are standing still, but it is otherwise functionless. The legs are short and in swimming the feet trail straight aft as rudders. The body is low in the water even when not wholly submerged, and as already fully noted, the wings are the propellors. In concordance with those arrangements, the normal stance when out of the water is with the body vertical, not balanced fore-and-aft of the feet but rising straight above them. It is this that gives penguins the ludicrous resemblance to little men on which their popularity largely depends.

Above the toes a penguin's legs have three segments, as in birds generally, but the proportions are quite different from those of almost all other birds. The uppermost segment, most heavily muscled, corresponds with our thigh and has the homologous bone, the femur. The next segment is also fairly well muscled; it is the drumstick of chickens. It is usually somewhat longer than the thigh and it corresponds approximately with our shin. It contains the tibia bone and the slender fibula, as in us, but the tibia also has fused with it some of the small bones that in us are separate ankle (tarsal) bones. For precision the main bone of this segment is therefore called the tibiotarsus in birds. Because of that fusion, the joint between shin and foot is not in the same position in birds and in mammals (such as us) but is more distal between ankle bones. The next segment involves the fusion into one bone of what are in mammals and were in the ancestors of birds a number of different bones, including the distal ankle bones (tarsals) and the remaining three metatarsals, the bones of the arches in our feet. (We have five, which was the primitive number for both avian and mammalian ancestors.) In almost all birds except penguins this complex bone, called the tarsometatarsus, is long and slender. In penguins it is short and wide. It is the most distinctive single bone in penguins. Once seen it can never be mistaken for a bone of any other bird, which is a blessing for paleontologists who have to identify birds and other vertebrate animals by their bones alone.

The shortness of the tarsometatarsus also makes the whole leg in penguins unusually short and contributes to their waddling way of walking. When standing still, penguins rest much of their weight on this segment, like a man with his heel on the ground although the hind end of this penguin segment does not exactly correspond with our heel. When penguins walk they get up on their toes, always three in number, all of which articulate directly with the single tarsometatarsal bone.

The peculiar stance and leg structure of penguins have also led to some odd secondary developments that are not present in all species and so are not part of the basic penguin but dependent on it. One of these is the habit of tobogganing, flopping onto the belly and shoving along on it, which on snow can be considerably faster than penguins' walking. Another is the possibility of incubating a single egg by holding it on the feet under a fold of flesh.

It is also consonant with their stance and their streamlining that penguins have short necks, so much so as to appear practically neckless, and that their heads face at right angles to the body, another manlike trait. Their bills differ considerably among the various species but are generally neither very long nor very slender. Differences in shape are correlated to some extent with food habits, but as far as known not very strongly or clearly.

All penguins feed exclusively on marine animals, and mostly on those that occur at relatively small depths in the ocean. That varies to some extent with the size of the species. As might be expected from their relatively great size, emperors tend to dive more deeply and to stay down longer than has been observed for other penguins. The record known dive for an emperor, observed only once so far, lasted a bit over eighteen minutes, but even for emperors the usual dive is under three minutes, and for them, as for other species on which good observations have been made, dives over six minutes in duration are exceptional. In most species longer dives have not been observed. Emperors also hold the record for depth, one having made an accurately measured dive to a depth of about 870 feet (265 meters). Again, that is highly exceptional even for an emperor. In emperors most dives, and in smaller species perhaps all dives (information is incomplete), are less than 65 or 70 feet (about 20 meters).

Penguin food is provided almost entirely by crustaceans, fishes, and squids. Some penguins will take almost any of these foods as they become available, but none can live indefinitely without seasonal abundance, at least, of one or another of the three kinds. Some do have dietary preferences, or habits. For example adélies and some other far southern species live mostly on krill (tiny crustaceans of the group called euphausiids) supplemented by very small fish, but magellanics feed mainly on squids, and blackfooted penguins mostly on fish of moderate size. It can be argued whether

3. *Sketch map of some of the geographic factors influencing the physical
environments, distribution, and ecology of penguins.* The oceanic features
noted are all quite variable and their representation is only approximate.
The convergences are bands of rising and sinking water masses and mark
changes in surface temperatures. Except for the adélies and emperors in
the far south and the Galápagos penguins on the equator, penguins are
almost confined to coasts and islands north of the Antarctic Circle and
south of the Tropic of Capricorn.

penguins eat what is available where they live or live where
what they eat is available. Probably the ancestral penguins
were omnivorous among small and medium-sized shallow-
water animal foods, and penguins later became secondarily
somewhat differentiated in food habits according to what was
abundant in regions to which particular species were confined for other largely physiological reasons.

Much penguin food, especially among the crustaceans, has
a high salt content, and exceptionally high salt intake has to
be coped with in some special way. In marine mammals that
is taken care of by large specialized kidneys. In penguins the
kidneys have not become particularly specialized and would
be inadequate by themselves. Salt secretion occurs largely
through a pair of glands that lie on top of the skull back of
the beak. These are so effective that penguins can even drink
sea water (fatal to us), without ill effects. That is clearly a
characteristic of the basic penguin, the more evidently so
because similar special salt glands occur in petrels, also
seabirds and probably related to the ancestry of penguins.

All birds are warm-blooded, generally more so than mammals, including men. That is also true of penguins. Although
under somewhat unusual conditions body temperatures as
low as about 91½° Fahrenheit (33° Centigrade) and as high
as about 107° F (41.7° C) have been recorded, more usual
temperatures seem to be in the range 100° F (37.8° C) to
102° F (38.9° C). Those are not high temperatures for birds.

Various species of penguins range from about 78°S latitude
to the equator and hence occur in a wide variety of environments and climates, although normally always within a few
miles, at most, of an ocean and in the oceans themselves
(Map 3). Nevertheless they rarely encounter air temperatures
and never water temperatures as warm as their own bodies.
Even those in the tropics usually frequent water that is relatively cool for those latitudes, notably the Benguela Current

off the west coast of Africa and the Humboldt Current off that of South America. In the Galápagos Islands farthest north and most tropical for penguins, the average year-round water temperature is about 73½° (23° C), still far below the penguins' temperature range. It is also noticeable there that the penguins tend to be more common in the west, where the water is usually cooler than around the eastern islands. At McMurdo Base in Antarctica, which at latitude 77°51′S approximates the southern limit for penguins, the hottest summer day ever recorded was 2 January 1974 when the air temperature reached 8.3° C (nearly 47° F). In winter the air temperatures there never go above freezing, average about −13° F (−25° C) and reach below −40° F (which happens also to be −40° C). Open water in comparable latitudes is generally at or somewhat below 30° F (about −1° C) the year around.

It is thus evident that penguins in general, which is to say the basic penguin, have problems of temperature control. That is clearly true for heat production and retention, but oddly enough it is also true for avoidance of overheating. The precise nature and intensity of the problems vary with environmental conditions, with extremes for the Galápagos penguins on the equator and the emperor penguins in Antarctica, but all penguins have adaptations for producing and both for retaining and for reducing body heat.

As for heat production, metabolic rates in penguins of course vary widely, both within and between species, but there is evidence that they are unusually high, as they are also in many marine mammals. There is an ample internal supply of heat, and there are adaptations for keeping undue amounts of this from being lost to the much cooler external environment.

Some adaptations for heat conservation are species-specific, not general or basic penguin characteristics. These may be behavioral. For example emperor penguins, both chicks and adults, but not those of more temperate climes, crowd together in tight groups or huddles, amusingly called turtles (*tortues*) by the French investigators. In other regions many penguins nest or spend much of their shore time in holes, small caves, crannies, or vegetations that are not available in the ice, frozen ground, and poorly vegetated Antarctic.

Other more bodily adaptations vary in extent in penguins of different environments but are present in all species. For example, all penguins are heavier than the vast majority of flying birds, but among the penguins there is a definite although irregular tendency for those exposed to greater cold to be heavier. That is a general rule, with various exceptions, among warm-blooded animals. It follows from a mechanical or thermodynamic fact. Although affected by other factors, notably insulation, heat loss tends to be proportional to the ratio of surface area to body volume, because the production and amount of heat varies with size and its loss varies with the surface over which radiation loss occurs. It is a geometrical relationship that the larger a body is, the lower its ratio of surface to volume. (If you don't like arithmetic, you have my permission to skip the rest of this paragraph.) This is easily exemplified by simple arithmetic. The volume of a sphere is given by $1/6(\pi d^3)$, where π is the familiar constant 3.1416 and d is the diameter. The area of the surface of a sphere is πd^2. Thus a sphere with diameter 1 centimeter, let us say (the unit doesn't matter), will have a volume of 0.52 cubic centimeter. Its surface will be 3.14 square centimeters. If the diameter is doubled, the volume becomes 4.19 and the surface 12.57. The volume has increased eight times and the surface only four times.

There is a good mathematical reason why the emperor penguins, which live in the coldest part of penguins' habitats, should average about 66 pounds (about 30 kilograms) in weight, and Galápagos penguins, living in the warmest part, only about 5 pounds (about 2¼ kilos). It is true that adélie penguins, which range as far south as emperors, average only about 11 pounds (about 5 kilos), but here a species-specific adaptive difference in behavior occurs. Emperor penguins stay in the far south to breed in the coldest weather, but adélies breed there only in summer and take to warmer seas in winter. Furthermore, the smallest of all (measured) penguins, the little blue penguins of Chatham Island, east of New Zealand, average only 2⅕ pounds (1 kilo) in weight, less than half the weight of the Galápagos penguins and yet they live farther south, around 44°S latitude. But members of the same species, not really appreciably larger, range farther north, to around 34°S, and into water little colder than in the west Galápagos.

Apart from behavior and weight, a bird's first defense against cold is its feathers, as a mammal's is its fur. Here the penguins are all peculiarly and excellently provided for. They are more completely covered with feathers than almost any other birds and, insignificant as most of the individual feathers may seem, they are ideal for their purpose. When the feathers are lying flat, the scalelike exposed parts overlap and form a surface practically impermeable to wind or water. Furthermore, on the shafts below them are tufts that form an insulating layer almost like eiderdown. A second line of defense is formed by a likewise insulating layer of fat or blubber over most of the body below the skin. (We will later see that this was a misfortune for some penguins because they used to be boiled down, or tried out, for their oil just as whales were.) It will be no surprise that the insulation varies with the usual environments. Species in colder climates have longer feathers and thicker blubber than those in warmer climates.

It is not surprising that penguins have adaptations for keeping warm. It is surprising that they also have adaptations for keeping cool and that one of the leading students of these birds, Bernard Stonehouse, to whose work I am constantly indebted, thinks that even in Antarctica keeping cool is a greater problem for penguins than keeping warm. He says,

> Imagine yourself dressed in a thick, well padded waterproof suit, and required alternately to rest for hours in cold water, swim violently and beat your way ashore through surf, run, fight, make love and build a house, and then return to the cold sea. Without special mechanisms for ventilating the suit you would alternate between chilling and apoplexy, and be thoroughly uncomfortable most of the time.

Indeed adélie penguins seem to suffer from the heat if the air temperature gets much above freezing. Tropical penguins can of course stand much warmer weather, but they usually manage to find shady places of one kind or another for their daylight hours ashore.

All penguins can increase heat radiation by ruffling their feathers, thus reducing their insulating power and exposing the skin. They also spread the wings, exposing more surface to the air. Radiation from the body is further increased by greater flow of warm blood into the blubber just under the surface. As would again be expected, species in relatively warm environments tend to have somewhat larger and more thinly feathered wings as radiating areas, and some bare patches on the head or around the feet. As would also be expected, adélies have unusually long feathers and are also the most completely covered with feathers of all penguins, perhaps of all birds. The feathers extend well out onto the beak, even covering what in other birds would be the openings of the nostrils. This is one of the peculiarities that makes this species so remarkable and unmistakable.

Penguins normally lay only one or two eggs, depending on the species, and among those that lay two, some usually incubate only one. Both parents usually take part in incubating the eggs and feeding the chicks. When these aspects of the lives of the various species are discussed later it will become obvious that it takes two adults to hatch and feed one or two chicks and that larger broods would be quite impossible.

It would be difficult to say anything more about penguins in general or the basic penguin. To another penguin each penguin is an individual and even to us, less discriminating, each species or sometimes even each local population has its own distinctive characteristics. It is, for example, meaningless to say how or where penguins in general make their nests, lay their eggs, or do many other things, because they do them in many different ways. Some of those will be discussed in following chapters. However, one further word should be said here about what is meant by the basic penguin. That means, or at least I use it to mean, the complex of essential characteristics common to all penguins and in that sense defining penguinness, as one might define the basic qualities of humanity without forgetting the infinite, and on the whole delightful, variations of men and women singly and as all mankind. The basic penguin is not the ancestral penguin, unknown alas! That ancestor, or rather that ancestral population, at some point almost certainly had the characteristics common to all penguins now living, but it certainly also had special characteristics of its own, just as each living species has. Some of those characteristics probably no longer exist in any present species. Others quite possibly persist in some and not in others. The same sort of thing could be said about any group of related organisms, including ourselves, *Homo sapiens*. That is one of the reasons for studying penguins.

1.   Adult emperor penguin and chick in juvenile plumage off Ross Island, Antarctica.

2–4. Adult emperor penguins off Ross Island, Antarctica.

5. King penguins, Macquarie Island.

6. Adélie penguin on Torgeson Island, Antarctica.

7.   Gentoos on New Island, Falklands.

8.   Young adélie penguins on Torgeson Island, Antarctica.

9. Galápagos penguin, Fernandina Island.

10. Rockhopper penguin with young, New Island, Falklands.

11. Little blue penguin.

12. Adélie penguin rookery, with adults and chicks, near Palmer Station, Antarctica.

13. Adélie penguin with two large chicks, Torgeson Island, Antarctica.

14–15. Adélie penguins feeding young, Torgeson Island, Antarctica.

16. Adélie penguins, adults and young on rocky nests, near Palmer Station, Antarctica.

17. Adult adélie with young moulting from down to first-year plumage, Torgeson Island, Antarctica.

18. King (left) and gentoo penguins on beach, Macquarie Island.

19. Gentoo penguins and rocky nests, Gonzalo Videla, Antarctica.

20.   Gentoo penguins and rich vegetation, Macquarie Island.

21.   A rookery with more than 100,000 rockhopper penguins on New Island, Falklands.

22. Blackfooted penguin with egg in a cranny along the coast of South Africa.

23. Rescue operations by SANCCOB in Cape Town to save blackfooted penguins oiled by spills at sea.

24.   Magellanic penguin, Falkland Islands.

4. Penguins Past

It has been recorded and regretted that we do not yet have any direct knowledge of the origin of penguins. In such cases the situation is not hopeless. Several more or less indirect approaches can usually lead to a plausible theory, at least, as to how any group of organisms arose. If the group is still well represented in the modern fauna, as penguins are, it is not difficult to determine what basic specializations were involved in the evolutionary origin of the group. That was done in the last chapter. The characters of the basic penguin were almost certainly present in the ancestral penguins as soon as they had achieved distinct differentiation as a group, a family and order in technical terms. The next step is to make broader comparisons and to see how those special characters most probably originated from more primitive conditions in other birds, for instance penguin flippers from the wings of aerial fliers. That will be done later in this chapter.

Another approach is to examine the known fossils, which are direct records of a part, at least, of the history of the group being studied. Although there are many reasons why the fossil record is still notoriously incomplete, it is always relevant to historical, evolutionary problems and in favorable instances already suffices to solve many of them. The origin of birds as a whole is virtually demonstrated by the circumstance, fortunate for us but unfortunate for them, that several creatures just in the transitional stage from reptiles to birds fell into Central European lagoons some 160 million years ago. They were buried in calcareous muds that became consolidated into lithographic limestone, and their remains were discovered by quarrymen in days, now past, when lithographs were ordinarily made on stone. They were named *Archaeopteryx* ("ancient wing") and have been studied in great detail.

Within the class of birds, the Aves, there has as yet been no such good fortune for penguins or a number of other groups. The transitional forms escaped fossilization or the fossils have not yet been found. Birds are not so likely to be preserved as fossils as are some other animals. Although a surprising number of fossil birds, including fossil penguins, have been discovered and studied, the record is spotty. That is especially true of the times and regions where the transitional and earliest penguins are most likely to have occurred. The transition from aerial ancestors probably occurred in the Cretaceous period, over 65 million years ago, and early differentiation and specialization probably extended through the Paleocene epoch, approximately 65 to 55 million years ago. Those evolutionary events were almost certainly confined to the southern hemisphere. But so far no fossil birds of any kind have been found in Paleocene, Cretaceous, or older rocks in the southern hemisphere. Birds certainly occurred there in those times and some almost certainly did become fossilized, but if so they have so far eluded discovery.

Table 1 shows the ages and places from which fossil penguins are now known.

No penguins more than 45 million years old have yet been discovered. That seems like a respectable age, and you might expect that penguins so old would be decidedly more primitive than those now living. In many respects that is not true, and indeed in some ways certain of the late Eocene penguins seem to be even more specialized, that is, less primitive, than those still extant. As far as their bones show, they were already completely adapted to the penguin way of life and had all the characteristics of the basic penguin plus some special characteristics of their own, different in the various species. At first sight that seems quite disappointing, and so it is to some ex-

Table 1.   Ages and Localities of Known Fossil Penguins

Geological ages		Approximate ages in years	Localities
Recent and Pleistocene		0–2,000,000	Scattered finds of recent species
Pliocene	Late	2,000,000–3,500,000	South Island, New Zealand; Cape Province, South Africa
	Early	3,500,000–5,500,000	
Miocene	Late	5,500,000–12,000,000	Victoria, Australia
	Middle	12,000,000–18,000,000	Patagonia (Chubut and Santa Cruz), Argentina; Cape Town, South Africa
	Early	18,000,000–25,000,000	
Oligocene	Late	25,000,000–30,000,000	South Island, New Zealand; South Australia
	Middle	30,000,000–33,000,000	North and South Islands, New Zealand
	Early	33,000,000–37,000,000	North and South Islands, New Zealand
Eocene	Late	37,000,000–45,000,000	South Australia; South Island, New Zealand; Seymour Island, Antarctica
	Middle	45,000,000–50,000,000	
	Early	50,000,000–55,000,000	(No known penguins earlier than late Eocene)
Paleocene		55,000,000–65,000,000	
Cretaceous		65,000,000 135,000,000	

tent, but it should not really be very surprising, and the fossils do have great interest even though they do not provide complete answers to questions about penguin origins.

Scrappy as the known fossil record for birds is, it is sufficient to indicate that all the orders of birds and most of the families had already become clearly differentiated by late Eocene times. They were then on an average rather more primitive than their modern relatives, but they had acquired the basic anatomical, and therefore in all probability also the physiological and behavioral, traits that distinguish modern orders and families. Therefore it is not strange that the same is true of penguins. The inference is that the great adaptive radiation of birds occurred mostly in the Cretaceous, was consolidated in the Paleocene, and was essentially over by the end of the Eocene. Cretaceous and Paleocene birds are still very poorly known, but knowledge of them in the northern hemisphere is increasing and it does support that view.

The distribution of known fossil penguins (Table 1) shows another interesting fact: all are from regions where penguins still occur. In fact their range in latitude is considerably less than for modern penguins, which, as already noted, range from as far south as there is now open sea water (about latitude 78°S) to the equator. The most southern locality for known fossil penguins is just off the coast of the Antarctic Peninsula, but at latitude 64°15'S it is well north of the Antarctic Circle and so is technically in the south temperate zone, astronomically speaking. The most northern known locality for fossil penguins is near Adelaide, South Australia, just south of latitude 35°S and in the south temperate zone by any definition (Map 4).

Another point not evident simply from the distribution table is that in all the regions where fossil penguins are known they were formerly more varied than penguins are there today, that is, sometime in the past there were more species in all those regions than there are now. From Seymour Island, Antarctica, five genera and six species of fossil penguins are known from rocks of the same age, now believed to be late Eocene although not absolutely certain. (Two more genera and species have been named, but they are doubtfully valid.) In the same general region only two genera and four species

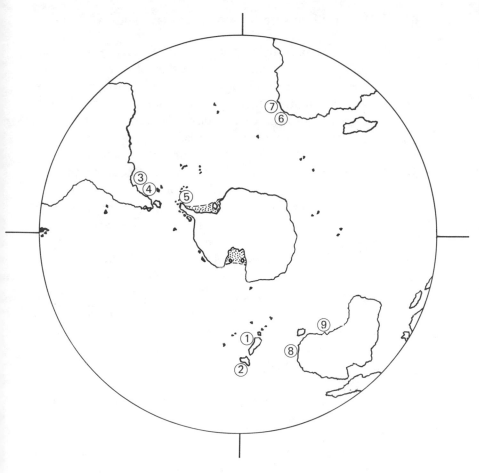

4. Localities of known fossil penguins.

1. South Island of New Zealand. Numerous localities; late Eocene to Pleistocene.
2. North Island of New Zealand. Three localities; Oligocene.
3. Chubut Valley, near Trelew, Argentina. Probably early Miocene.
4. San Julián, Argentina. Probably early Miocene.
5. Seymour Island (called Marambio in Argentina). Probably late Eocene.
6. Cape Town, South Africa. Probably Miocene.
7. Langebaanweg, South Africa. Pliocene.
8. Victoria, Australia. Three localities; Miocene.
9. South Australia. Two localities; Eocene and Oligocene.

(adélies, gentoos, chinstraps, and emperors) now occur. From Patagonia four genera and nine species of fossil penguins contemporaneous with each other in the early Miocene have been clearly distinguished, but only one species (magellanics) normally frequents that region now. In New Zealand the known fossil penguins cover an unusual age span, but for a single age (in the Oligocene) there are at least four genera and five species. In the same region of New Zealand there is now normally only one species (little blues), although for the whole of New Zealand there are three genera and four species (yellow-eyed, fiordland, little blue, white-flippered— the distinctness of the last somewhat dubious). The fossil penguins of Australia are less well known, but among fossils of one age (late Miocene) there are at least two genera and three species. Only one species (little blues) lives in that region now. African fossil penguins are even more poorly known, but a small collection from a single deposit of probable early Miocene age includes at least two species and possibly two genera. Here, too, there is only one resident recent species (blackfooted or jackass).

Those discrepancies become even more striking when it is realized that we surely know only a small fraction of the species of penguins that must have existed through geological times. At times in the past there evidently were many more species of penguins, both in general and in particular regions, than there are now. Most of them have become extinct. The word "extinct" is confusingly used in two different senses. We call some species extinct even though they have living descendants, if those descendants have changed enough in the course of evolution to go by a different name. Such species have not been annihilated. Their lineages have not terminated, and they are extinct only in a special and somewhat formal or arbitrary sense of the word. On the other hand innumerable species, many more than have survived in any form, have become extinct in the fullest sense. They have been annihilated; they have died off without progeny.

All the known fossil penguins that lived before the Pleistocene or Ice Age—that is, more than about two million years ago—are of species extinct in one sense or another of that word. All but two also belong to extinct genera. The two exceptions happen to be among the latest in age, geologically speaking (late Pliocene); there will be something more to say about them later. Close study of the remains of the other older species indicates that almost all of them became extinct completely, in the fullest sense. Somewhat unexpectedly, none of them can be definitely determined as ancestral to particular genera or species of modern penguins, and most of them can be fairly certainly ruled out as such ancestors. What has happened to remains of those ancestors? Well, the southern hemisphere, in which they must have lived, is vast, and its lands were even more extensive in the past. The places where fossil penguins have so far been found are only a handful of dots on the map. Further exploration will surely turn up more fossil penguins, and among them perhaps some ancestral ones. It is, however, likely that many or most of the ancestors of our present species evolved on and around islands where their remains were unlikely to be fossilized and still less likely to be discovered. Moreover, most of the older and smaller islands have probably disappeared completely, ending any chance of finding fossils of the organisms that evolved on them. Note that, except for an occasional stray, ten of the eighteen present species of penguins live only on islands and all the others also frequent islands without being quite confined to them.

Thus the history of penguins as we know it is marked by fairly early specialization, by repeated proliferation of numerous species most of which became extinct, and finally by the origin at unknown dates and eventual dominance of the eighteen species now living. The reason for the extinction of so many ancient penguins is not known. In fact a precise reason for past extinctions, for example that of the dinosaurs, is not really known in any case although there are often plenty of theories, some rather far-fetched. The general reason is always that some environmental change occurred and that the doomed species was physiologically and genetically unable to cope with the change. The usually insoluble problem is to determine just what the environmental change was and why the species could not cope with it. At least one popular theory can here be ruled out: humans have had nothing to do with the extinction of any known species of penguin. The extinct species known from fossils lived and died before humans had evolved as such. No recent species has become extinct although, as will be discussed later (in Chapter 8), at least one is in danger as a result of human activities.

For some of the ancient species there is one fairly plausible theory about their extinction, or perhaps it is better to call it a speculative hypothesis. In the early Miocene and earlier, some 20 to 45 million years ago, there were a number of unusually large penguins, none known in later times and none ancestral to living species. Around the time when they were becoming extinct the numbers of small cetaceans (such as dolphins and porpoises) and seals in the oceans were increasing. Many of them probably ate much the same food as the big penguins, and some of them probably ate the big penguins themselves. It is possible, at least, that the increased pressure of combined competition and predation had something to do with the extinction of those penguins. Nevertheless, some penguins as small as those now living also became extinct then, but the living species cope successfully with nonhuman competition and predation. This brings up the subject of the size of prehistoric penguins, to which we now turn.

There is a widespread idea that prehistoric animals in

general were gigantic. This probably arose from popular accounts of mammoths and of dinosaurs, although it was not altogether true even of them. Mammoths came in assorted sizes, but even the largest of them was not much larger than the biggest African elephants, which they resembled and to which they were related. Some dinosaurs were exceptionally large, it is true, but there were small dinosaurs as well, and the largest animals that ever lived are still living. They are the blue whales, now near extinction from ruthless pursuit by man.

Stories of immense prehistoric penguins also have some truth but are also commonly exaggerated. The very first fossil penguin made known, by Thomas Henry Huxley as told in the first chapter of this book, was represented only by one incomplete bone but this indicated a size larger than the largest living penguins, the emperors. Huxley estimated the height of his species *Palaeeudyptes antarcticus* to have been between four and five feet, four being a reasonable estimate, five a bit high but not outrageously so. Unreasonable estimates soon followed, and heights up to seven feet are claimed even in ostensibly authoritative works still in print.

It is not easy to make such estimates on a reasonable scientific basis. For one thing, no complete skeleton of an extinct species of penguin has ever been found. Only three known specimens, one from Patagonia (Argentina) and two from New Zealand, include considerable parts of a single individual and they barely suffice for reconstruction of the skeleton as a whole. In general, then, and indeed even for those specimens, the overall size must be judged from the sizes of particular single bones, especially the upper wing bone (humerus), upper leg bone (femur), and main foot bone (tarsometatarsus). That has to be done on the premise that the ratios of the lengths of those bones to the heights of the birds as a whole were about as in living penguins. There is the further problem that those ratios vary from bone to bone and from species to species among recent penguins and doubtless did so also among the extinct ones. Then there is the added difficulty that what we really want to know about the size of a penguin is how tall it was when standing up, and accurate, technical studies of recent penguins never give that figure. They give only the total body length, with the body in quite an unnatural pose, which is not at all the same as the standing height.

With all those problems, it is not possible to give anything like an exact figure for the standing height of fossil penguins. Nevertheless I have been able to work out what I think are reasonable estimates for probable limits in those heights as far as estimates can be made on the available bones. The whole roster has never been published, so I give it here in Table 2. Some of the figures that have been published before are now somewhat modified. It is scientifically more acceptable to give these heights in centimeters, and they were calculated in the metric system. I have nevertheless transposed them into feet and inches as more familiar to most readers. To put them back into centimeters, change them to inches and then multiply them by 2.54.

Table 2 shows that most known fossil penguins were within the size range of the living species. Only two are at all likely to have been over five feet high, and the highest reasonable (somewhat improbable) figure is 5 feet 7 inches for *Anthropornis nordenskjoeldi* from Seymour Island. The largest of the fossil New Zealand penguins, *Pachydyptes ponderosus*, was about the same size or possibly a bit shorter, 5 feet 4 inches at most. These, decidedly the largest known penguins, have fairly descriptive technical names. *Anthropornis* means man-bird, and *nordenskjoeldi* is named for the famous polar explorer Otto Nordenskjöld, leader of the expedition on which the first specimens of this large penguin were found. (The actual collector, in 1903, was Gunnar Andersson.) *Pachydyptes* means

Table 2.   Estimates of Standing Heights of Extinct Penguins

Late Eocene
  New Zealand
    Pachydyptes ponderosus — 4'8"–5'4"
    Palaeeudyptes marplesi — 3'6"–4'9"
  Seymour Island
    Anthropornis nordenskjoeldi — 5'0"–5'7"
    Palaeeudyptes gunnari — 3'8"–4'1"
    Wimanornis seymourensis — 3'6"–3'11"
    Delphinornis larseni — 2'9"–3'1"
    Archaeospheniscus wimani — 2'5"–2'10"
Early Oligocene
  New Zealand
    Palaeeudyptes antarcticus — 3'8"–4'1"
    Archaeospheniscus lopdelli — 3'2"–4'
    Archaeospheniscus lowei — 2'9"–3'9"
    Platydyptes novaezealandiae — 2'9"–3'1"
    Duntroonornis parvus — 1'7"–2'4"
Late Oligocene
  New Zealand
    Platydyptes amiesi — 3'1"–3'6"
    Korora oliveri — 2'1"–2'5"
Early Miocene
  Argentina
    Arthrodytes grandis — 3'11"–4'5"
    Paraptenodytes antarcticus — 2'11"–3'4"
    Paraptenodytes robustus — 2'4"–2'8"
    Palaeospheniscus wimani — 2'4"–2'8"
    Palaeospheniscus patagonicus — 2'1"–2'5"
    Palaeospheniscus bergi — 1'11"–2'3"
    Palaeospheniscus gracilis — 1'9"–2'
Late Pliocene
  New Zealand
    Pygoscelis tyreei — 2'4"–2'8"
    Aptenodytes ridgeni — 3'0"–3'4"
Largest and smallest Recent penguins for comparison
    Aptenodytes forsteri (emperor) — About 3'3"
    Eudyptula minor (little blue) — About 1'2"

heavy diver, and *ponderosus* means just what it sounds like, "ponderous." *Pachydyptes ponderosus* had unusually stout bones and was probably heavier than *Anthropornis nordenskjoeldi* whether quite as tall or not.

The fossil penguins averaged somewhat larger than recent penguins—the average standing height for all eighteen living species is only about two feet—and none yet discovered is as small as the smallest living species (see below). That may, however, be an accident of preservation, collecting, or both.

A comparison of sizes. Left to right: six-foot man; largest known extinct penguin; largest living penguin (emperor); smallest known penguin (little blue, living); guillemot (one of the living auks that can fly in both air and water); least auklet (smallest auk). Scale at left in feet.

Large fossils are easier to see than small ones, and only for Patagonia do we have large enough collections to be at all likely to represent the original range of sizes. Most of the extinct Patagonian species are around the size of penguins still living in those latitudes, although one, *Paraptenodytes antarcticus*, was probably between a king and an emperor in size and one, *Arthrodytes grandis*, was larger. It is known only by a few scraps from the southernmost locality for fossil penguins in Patagonia, and they may represent strays from still farther south.

This discussion has become somewhat prosy and may be telling you more about the sizes of fossil penguins than you care to know. Perhaps I can pick up the interest with another figure. If *Anthropornis nordenskjoeldi* had a standing height of 5 feet 4 inches, which is quite likely, it probably weighed around 300 pounds when reasonably well nourished. As penguins in general are not timid toward humans, a large man would have done well to avoid one of those birds—but there were then no men around.

In the last chapter I noted that in a somewhat irregular way there is a tendency for penguins to be larger in colder and smaller in warmer regions and that this can be at least partly explained by the mathematical relationship between body weight and surface area. It would of course be reasonable to suppose that Antarctica was even colder than today when the giant *Anthropornis nordenskjoeldi* lived there, New Zealand colder in the heyday of *Pachydyptes ponderosus*, and perhaps also Patagonia when *Arthrodytes grandis* either lived or strayed there. Curiously enough, that seems not to be true. There is a good bit of uncertainty in attempts to determine past climates and water temperatures, but approximations can often be made in various ways.

Penguins cannot live without access to open (unfrozen) sea water, and the Antarctic seas could not be appreciably colder than they are now without freezing. On those grounds alone it is obvious that the large fossil penguins of Seymour Island were not frequenting colder water than the present smaller Antarctic penguins. Also fossil plants from Seymour Island clearly indicate much warmer land and air conditions than at present, but the plants probably were not exactly contemporaneous with the penguins.

Under favorable conditions it is possible to estimate ancient sea temperatures by the ratio of different forms (isotopes) of oxygen in fossil shells. That ratio varies with water temperature, and it is preserved in shells that were being formed at the same time and incorporating oxygen derived from the surrounding water. That technique has been extensively applied in New Zealand, and it indicates a water temperature of almost 70° F (20° C) in the late Eocene, dropping to a bit under 55° F (about 12° C) in the Oligocene, the times when unusually large penguins were most common there. The latter temperature is near that of the sea off the east coast of the South Island now, but both temperatures are decidedly higher than those where king or, especially, emperor penguins now normally live.

There is as yet no direct check on sea temperatures in Patagonia when the known fossil penguins lived there, but land faunas, mostly mammals, are known from the same region at about the same time and they strongly suggest a warmer climate than the present one.

Recent penguins as large as emperors and kings never live in climates and seas as warm as is indicated for those still larger fossil penguins. It therefore is highly probable that the extinct penguins of equal or even greater size had a different system of heat balance and regulation. Possibly they had lower metabolic rates and possibly they tolerated higher body temperatures, but it is also probable that they were less insulated and had more extensive means of radiating heat.

Three late Pliocene penguins, perhaps about 2.5 million years old and so quite late in penguin history, are known from the South Island of New Zealand. They belong to three different genera and species. One is not closely related and surely not ancestral to any living genus or species. Of the others, one is similar both in size and structure to the living emperor penguins and the other similar in size and structure to the living gentoo penguins. The interesting point is that at latitude 43°S they lived, or at least died, far north of any area now normally visited by either emperors or gentoos. The most northern latitude for breeding emperors is about 66°S,

although a possibly demented stray did once land at the
southern end of New Zealand. The usual farthest north for
gentoos is about 46°S. In the late Pliocene the Ice Age was
approaching and water temperatures had dropped into the
50s Fahrenheit (some 10°–12° Centigrade), but that still is
too warm for emperors and gentoos now. Yet these fossils
were very like emperors and gentoos and possibly even
ancestral to the latter.

From their bones it is clear that all known fossil penguins
walked and swam in the same queer ways as modern penguins.
From their occurrence we know that they were also strictly
oceanic. Almost all known fossil penguins have been found
in rocks that were originally laid down as sediments in a
sea, as is indicated by the shells and other marine fossils also
found in them. Some may have been washed out to sea from a
nearby shore, but most, perhaps all of them, evidently died at
sea. That seems to be the usual final fate of adult penguins
today, and no doubt it has been so throughout their history.
A number of the fossil bones of penguins have tooth marks
on them, signs of the predators who ended their lives. The
only exception to burial at sea so far discovered is represented
by a small collection of penguin bones found in a late Pliocene
deposit at a place called Langebaanweg in Cape Province.
The sediment in which they were buried contains remains
of many land animals and evidently was deposited on land,
but the place was near the sea, as indicated by the presence
also of remains of seals.

Penguins do of course spend considerable time on land
but their rookeries or other breeding places are rarely sites
where sediment is being deposited, burying their remains—
the usual requisite for preservation as fossils. An isolated
penguin will occasionally wander a surprisingly long distance
from the shore. An example of such curious, unexplained
behavior is an adélie penguin that was found by a surveying

party in Antarctica in November 1973, one hundred miles from the nearest open water. That fortunate bird was taken to camp by toboggan and then flown to Adelaide Island, where there is an adélie rookery, and released. In the absence of surveyors such wrong-headed strays must die, for there is no penguin food outside of the ocean. Such incidents must always have been rare and sporadic. They have not led to discoveries of fossil penguins in other than marine or in just one case coastal deposits.

Although the known fossil penguins were already quite specialized not only in the basic penguin way but also in their own various specific ways, they do cast some light on penguin ancestry. The oldest known penguin skull, found by Justino Hernández of my exploring party in Patagonia in 1933, is only about 20 or 25 million years old, hence not old geologically speaking even as fossil penguins go. It belongs to *Paraptenodytes antarcticus*, a species that was rather large and also somewhat specialized in several other respects. Nevertheless some features of its skull and jawbones were distinctly more primitive than in any living penguin. In some of the skeletal bones of the older known fossil penguins there are also primitive features. For example, on an average the tarsometatarsal bones (described in the previous chapter) are more elongated and more firmly fused than in living penguins. These are resemblances to aerial flying birds. Some of these older and evidently somewhat primitive features of the fossils are also resemblances to a particular group of aerial birds: the order Procellariiformes, including the albatrosses, fulmars, shearwaters, petrels, and their relatives.

The fossil record of the Procellariiformes is inadequate and is of little help for the present enquiry. There is still the other approach: comparison and interpretation of resemblances in anatomy, physiology, and behavior of extant birds. Such studies have been carried out in great detail, especially by the great German zoologist Fürbringer as early as 1888 and continuing down to the present. There has been some argument, but a strong, now almost complete consensus has finally developed. It is generally agreed that among other recent birds the penguins, that is, the Sphenisciformes, resemble the Procellariiformes more than any others. Such resemblances can be due to convergent evolution, which is the result of adaptation to similar ways of life. The Sphenisciformes and the Procellariiformes are all oceanic birds and a few Procellariiformes even fly underwater in a penguinlike way. Nevertheless, convergence can be pretty well ruled out as a main cause of the resemblance. That resemblance is especially close anatomically for some Procellariiformes that are not so closely similar to penguins in mode of life, the shearwaters for example. Moreover the anatomical resemblance is decidedly less close for the murres, auks, and their allies in the order Charadriiformes, although many of these birds are more penguinlike in habits and (as we noted for the late great auk) in superficial appearance than any Procellariiformes.

It is probable that the Procellariiformes are in fact the closest living relatives of the Sphenisciformes, which is another way of saying that these two groups probably had a common ancestry that was distinct from the ancestry of any other living order of birds. Because birds in general evolved as aerial flyers and the Procellariiformes continue to be such, their common ancestors with the Sphenisciformes were aerial flyers also. Thus the Procellariiformes probably are somewhat more like that ancestry. However, it is wildly improbable that any living procellariiform really closely resembles the common ancestor with the penguins, which can hardly have lived more recently than 65 million years ago and probably a good bit less recently. If we knew that ancestor, as we do not but still may some day, we surely would not call it a penguin or a spherisciform. Whether we would call it a procellariiform is doubtful and not particularly important.

Why did the penguins make this radical change in locomotion and various other more or less associated ways of life while their now not very close relatives continued more in the old ways? A reasonable answer can be given, facilitated by the facts that a similar change has also occurred two other times independently and that some living birds are even now in an adaptively intermediate phase.

Two fairly specific theories on this subject were already advanced in the 19th century, but later knowledge makes it necessary to reject both. One of the discarded theories held that ancestral pre-penguins never flew but were bipeds with reptilelike front legs. It was supposed that they then took to the water, as has happened with various land animals, and that the front legs became adapted as flippers. As already sufficiently noted here, there is overwhelming evidence that penguins had aerial flying ancestors, and that conclusively refutes this theory.

The second theory had it that the pre-penguins became nonflying running birds, something like ostriches in habits but probably considerably smaller. It was then supposed that some of those land birds took to the ocean, impelled perhaps by deterioration of Antarctic climates or perhaps by proliferation of predators. No longer having functional wings, they evolved flippers, and they survived when their land relatives became extinct. But the anatomical evidence makes it abundantly clear that the ancestors of the penguins never did lose the use of their wings. It is inconceivable that they became ostrichlike and then evolved anew a complete set of flight muscles with their attachments and mechanical arrangements exactly as in aerial birds. Moreover, living examples in other groups make it quite clear how the transition from aerial to aquatic flying not only could but also must have occurred without any intervening truly flightless phase.

Both of the two instances of separate evolution of an almost fully penguinlike way of life have already been mentioned.

One is of course the recently extinct great auk, the original "penguin." It was very closely related to the common auks and is always classified in the same family (Alcidae), sometimes in the same genus (*Alca*), although more commonly in a separate genus of its own (*Pinguinus*, an adaptation of its original popular name). The other example is provided by a group of extinct Pacific coast birds, more distantly related to the auks, sometimes classified as a subfamily (Mancallinae) of the same family (Alcidae) and sometimes as a separate family (Mancallidae). Two genera and four species are known, ranging from late Miocene to middle Pliocene in age. The point is that both the great auk and the older extinct Pacific group independently lost aerial flight and continued with aquatic flight only. Yet both, in different degrees, are related to birds that have both aerial and aquatic flight, which in turn are related to birds that have only aerial flight. It is obvious that no truly flightless, entirely terrestrial stage was involved in their evolution.

The birds with both aerial and aquatic flight illustrate a middle term in that functional evolutionary sequence. Such birds occur both among the Charadriiformes, auks and their allies, and among the Procellariiformes, especially interesting in this connection because of an ancestral relationship to pre-penguins. Among these the diving petrels (family Pelecanoididae—not related to pelicans) are perhaps the most instructive for present purposes. For example the species called *potoyunco* in Peru, *Pelecanoides garnotii* scientifically, nests in burrows, as many penguins do in places where digging is not too difficult, fly by air somewhat laboriously to feeding grounds at sea, then pursue their food—small crustaceans and fishes as with many penguins—by aquatic flight, again as with penguins. Moreover in this species, extensively studied by the late Robert Cushman Murphy, the wing quills (pinions or flight feathers) are all molted at the same time. Until they grow again the birds continue to feed at sea, but they travel away from land by aquatic flight only. It appears that they are on the verge of becoming completely penguinlike. These are not a survival of the penguin ancestry, but surely they resemble the transitional stage in that ancestry.

The birds with both aerial and aquatic flight are on a threshold of potential change, but they are also adaptively stable under existing conditions. Their labored whirring aerial flight is less efficient than that of most exclusively aerial birds, and their aquatic flight is less prolonged and probably less efficient than that of exclusively aquatic birds, but both are adequate and the two fit together into a viable pattern of adaptation. The shape and size of the wing is necessarily a compromise between what would be best in the two quite different media in which it is used. The crucial point would come when aquatic flight became definitely more important and aerial flight dispensable. This shift in the direction of natural selection is evidently associated with increase in size. The great auk, as its name implies, was much larger than any auk that retained aerial flight (see diagram, p. 68). The smallest penguins are decidedly larger than the largest diving petrels and of about the same size as the largest auks with aerial flight. Penguins of average size, even today, are heavier than all but a few aerial (gliding) birds, and the larger living penguins are much heavier than any aerial birds now existing or known ever to have existed.

All the changes that occurred as penguins evolved from their flying ancestors made them less and less like those ancestors in particular, less like primitive early birds in general, and less like the majority of surviving birds. Somehow a legend has persisted that penguins are themselves primitive birds, or even the most primitive of all living birds. This simply is not true. They are among the most specialized, hence least primitive, of all birds, living or extinct.

5. Penguins Present

The stunning diversity of living things on the earth and their progressive development for over three billion years so far have depended on evolutionary processes among which speciation is basic. Speciation occurs when two populations cease to interbreed and each goes its way. Thereafter the two now separate species diverge by other evolutionary processes, notably mutation, recombination of genetic units in the population, and natural selection. Among animals distinctly perceptive of each other, as birds notably are, it is important and often essential that there be some way in which they recognize which others belong to their own species. These are the ones with which it is biologically proper to breed or in general to associate. The means of recognition are quite varied in different groups. Recognition may be purely by behavioral or vocal cues, even by apparently unconscious stimulation. In birds, highly visual animals, it is usually by sight.

So it is in penguins. They recognize their own species mainly by patterns of the head and upper body, readily visible even when they are swimming partly submerged. Once when I expounded on this to an audience I was severely criticized for being racist. That was utterly nonsensical. These are merely among the ethically neutral facts of nature, besides being biologically necessary. Furthermore I was talking about species, not races, and that is an essential distinction. All humans belong to a single species, which they, too, recognize by sight, and therefore it is perfectly proper biologically for any two humans of opposite sexes to breed together. Whether it is always proper in other respects is not a matter that concerns us here.

We are also dominantly visual animals, and we, too, can usually distinguish species of penguins readily by their head and upper body patterns. Groups of species that have become differentiated relatively recently have generally similar but not identical patterns. In classification these groups are designated as genera, and it is impossible for anyone, even a human, to mistake one genus for another. Species belonging to the same genus have minor distinctions which are particularly clear between species that are in frequent contact. Those rarely or never in contact have had less selective pressure to evolve clear specific clues. This is most evident in the genus *Eudyptes*, some species of which may be hard for humans to distinguish. In fact there is some evidence of occasional mistakes by the penguins themselves.

In this chapter I will deal with the recognition marks, distribution, and some peculiarities of each species. Later chapters will treat of some special aspects of life among the various species. Although they were introduced by name in Chapter 3, it may be convenient to list the living genera and species here for reference (Colorplates 1, 2).

Genus *Aptenodytes*
    Aptenodytes forsteri   Emperor penguins
    Aptenodytes patagonicus   King penguins
Genus *Pygoscelis*
    Pygoscelis antarctica   Chinstrap penguins
    Pygoscelis papua   Gentoo penguins
    Pygoscelis adeliae   Adélie penguins
Genus *Megadyptes*
    Megadyptes antipodes   Yellow-eyed penguins
Genus *Spheniscus*
    Spheniscus magellanicus   Magellanic penguins
    Spheniscus humboldti   Peruvian penguins
    Spheniscus demersus   Blackfooted penguins
    Spheniscus mendiculus   Galápagos penguins

Genus *Eudyptes*
    Eudyptes chrysolophus   Macaroni penguins
    Eudyptes crestatus   Rockhopper penguins
    Eudyptes sclateri   Erect-crested penguins
    Eudyptes schlegeli   Royal penguins
    Eudyptes pachyrhynchus   Fiordland penguins
    Eudyptes robustus   Snares Island penguins
Genus *Eudyptula*
    Eudyptula minor   Little blue penguins
    Eudyptula albosignata   White-flippered penguins

Aptenodytes forsteri, the emperor penguin, has been weighed in at 42 to 101½ pounds (19 to 46 kilos), averages about 66 pounds (30 kilos), making it much the largest of penguins and among the heaviest of all birds (Figs. 1–4). It is distinguished both by its size and by the bright yellow upper part of its breast, connecting with a so-called ear patch on the side of the otherwise black head. The back is a somewhat bluish gray and the breast, below the yellow, is white as in all penguins. These birds breed in winter on shelf or floe ice along the coasts of Antarctica; two colonies have now been found breeding on pebble beaches. In those places they can make no nests, so the single egg is held on the feet sheltered by a fold of abdominal skin. The male goes without eating during one or two months of courtship and then incubates the egg for about two months, during which he has nothing to eat—one reason for the marked variation in weight. Meanwhile the female is feeding at sea and finally comes back and regurgitates some of her banquet to the newborn chick while the male at last goes off to break his fast. In the spring the chicks go to sea on broken bits of floe ice, finally taking to the water when they have molted and replaced their fluff. The whole family spends the summer at sea, sometimes far from land or fixed ice (Map 5).

Aptenodytes patagonicus, the king penguins, weigh about half as much as emperor penguins. They are similarly marked

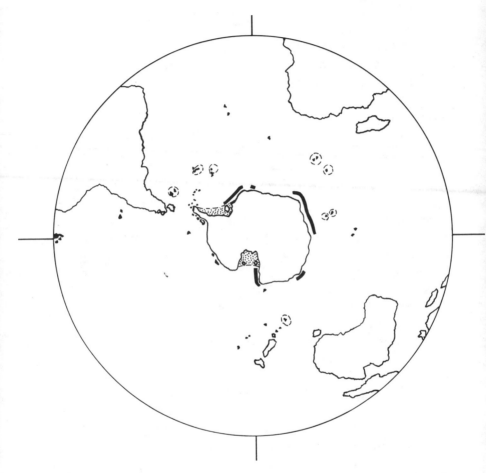

5. *Distribution of breeding colonies of emperor and king penguins.* The colonies are on the coasts, or in the case of the emperors on shelf ice, within or opposite the symbols shown: ▬▬ emperors (*Aptenodytes forsteri*); – – – – kings (*A. patagonicus*).

but the ear patch is more vivid, rather orange than yellow, and to my eyes they are the most handsome of all penguins. Emperors and kings may occasionally meet at sea or when far-straying, but they breed in entirely different places so that great difference in recognition marks has not evolved. The kings breed well to the north of Antarctica, on sub-antarctic and cold temperate islands, in a large circle from Tierra del Fuego (where they formerly occurred but are now rare or extinct) through the Falklands, South Georgia, South Sandwich, Marion, Crozet, Kergulen, and Heard Islands and clear around to Macquarie Island, southeast of Australia and southwest of New Zealand (Fig. 5). They occupy low, often marshy places near the shores, and there incubate a single egg in the same way as the emperors. Nearby open water occurs in their environment the year around, so that male and female can take turns incubating the egg and feeding the chick. The chicks are born in late spring or early summer but hang around all summer and the following winter, not going off on their own until they are about a year old. That oddly throws the breeding out of cycle, as will be further discussed in Chapter 6.

The three species of *Pygoscelis* have different ranges, but these overlap and all three may even be seen locally within a single rookery if you are fortunate enough to visit the far south (Map 6). They all have neat black and white suits, but as would be expected from the overlap of their breeding ranges their heads have distinct patterns recognizable at almost any distance. In the best-known penguin, *Pygoscelis adeliae*, the head is all black and the black feathers even extend over much of what is, in other species, the exposed posterior part of the bill (Figs. 6, 7, 8). The bill is dark in color. In the gentoo, *Pygoscelis papua*, the head is also mainly black but the bill is more exposed and is yellow, and there is a white band across the top of the head from one eye to the

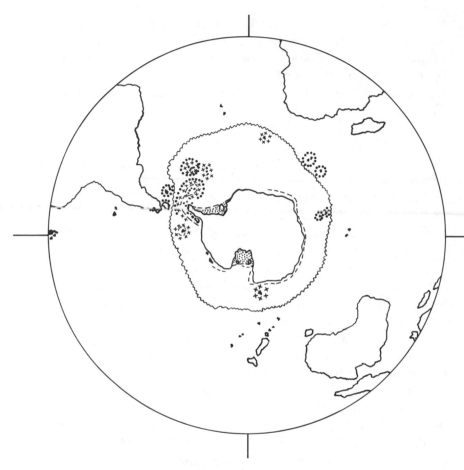

6. *Distribution of breeding colonies of* Pygoscelis *penguins, indicated as on Map 5.* The approximate position of the Antarctic Convergence is added, showing that these penguins are almost confined to coasts along the colder waters south of the convergence.

× × × × Chinstrap (*P. antarctica*)
• • • • • • Gentoo (*P. papua*)
– – – Adélie (*P. adeliae*)
〜〜〜 Approximate position of the Antarctic Convergence

other. The chinstrap penguin, *Pygoscelis antarctica*, has only the top and back of the head black, the area around the eyes, chin, and cheek being white, and there is a thin black stripe running from the back of the cap around the chin (Fig. 7).

The adélies have an extraordinarily wide breeding range, from about as far south as the emperors (at Cape Royds on Ross Island at over 77°30′S) up to the tip of the Antarctic Peninsula and beyond to the South Shetland, South Orkney, and South Sandwich Islands and even to Bouvetøy Island, which is beyond the limit of pack ice. The gentoos also breed on the northern part of the Antarctic Peninsula and from there on north also over an extraordinarily wide range, the more northern Antarctic, most of the subantarctic islands, and still in force up to the Falklands. The breeding range of the chinstrap penguins is almost identical with the northern part of the adélies' range, from about latitude 65°S northward through the nominally Antarctic islands of the western sector. (By nominally Antarctic I mean south of the Antarctic convergence, where warmer water comes to the surface, but north of the Antarctic circle.) There is thus also considerable overlap with the southern range of the gentoos, but gentoos do not extend quite so far south as chinstraps. It is unlikely that any two of these three species evolved in just the same area. They probably evolved on different islands or island groups and later came to occupy some of the same regions as the populations expanded. That would have occurred after they had diverged sufficiently to restrict or stop interbreeding. Their present sharply developed recognition patterns probably became emphasized after the overlap of ranges had happened.

Adélies average about 11 pounds (5 kilos) in weight, chinstraps about 10 pounds (4½ kilos), and gentoos about 12 to 13½ pounds (5½ to 6 kilos) in different parts of their range. As many of these populations live in the same environments, it is not surprising that the differences in size are moderate. It is, however, somewhat anomalous that the most northern gentoos, in the least cold environments, are the largest, although even that difference is not great. All three species are colonial and nest in rookeries, which may include thousands of individuals. All normally nest on the ground and lay two eggs, incubating both. In the south the nests are slight hollows, built up with pebbles. The most northern gentoos may use grass and twigs, and some even nest on top of clumps of tussock grass, although in one of their northernmost occurrences, in the Falklands, I have seen somewhat naive youngsters making nests with lumps of hard clay.

Megadyptes antipodes, the yellow-eyed penguin, averages about 11 pounds (about 5 kilos) in weight, somewhat above the mean for penguins in general. There is only one species in this genus and it looks quite unlike the species of any other genus so has no identity problem. These penguins have yellow catlike eyes and largely yellow heads with black streaks. They live along the shore in clumps of tussock grass around the southern end of the South Island of New Zealand and smaller islands on southward so far as Campbell Island in latitude 52°30'S (Map 7). They seldom stray, usually staying in nearby waters and rarely going to sea for longer than a week or so at a time even when not incubating or feeding young. They lay two eggs every year, incubate them in hidden nests on the ground for about six weeks, and commonly raise both chicks if not molested, as those along the shores of New Zealand proper often are. Although they are hardly known outside of New Zealand, they are famous among students of penguins because one of the most eminent students of these birds, the New Zealand zoologist L. E. Richdale, made a series of remarkable studies of this species. There are almost no Maoris in their range now, but when there were the Maoris called them *hoiho*, which I like much better

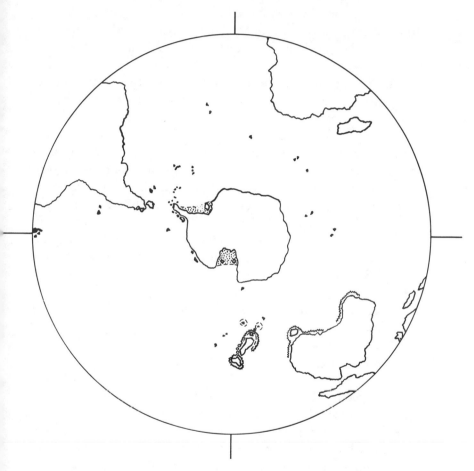

7. *Distribution of breeding colonies of* Megadyptes *and* Eudyptula *penguins, indicated as on Map 5.*

– – – Yellow-eyed (*M. antipodes*)
〰〰〰 Little blue or fairy (*E. minor*)
∘∘∘∘∘∘ White-flippered (*E. albosignata*)

than "yellow-eyed penguin." (The surviving Maoris are almost all on the North Island, where there are no hoihos.)

The four species of the genus *Spheniscus* are so much alike that their separation must have occurred fairly recently, geologically speaking, at least. They do have recognition marks, but these are not very obvious at a glance and are not often needed, as it is unusual now for any two of the species to come into much contact on their breeding grounds. All have black heads, with a white mark circling from above each eye, back, down, and forward around the neck and up the other side. Below this mark on the neck the magellanic penguin, *Spheniscus magellanicus*, has a rather broad black band or collar that merges at the shoulder into the black back. Below that again is another black stripe across the chest and extending down each flank (Fig. 24). Thus below the black chin there are two black stripes. This species breeds from near latitude 42°S in Patagonia (southern Argentina) around the tip of South America and up the Pacific side to about the latitude of Valparaiso (33°05'S), not exclusively but mostly on islands, including Tierra del Fuego and the Falklands, or Malvinas as the Argentinians, who claim but do not occupy them, prefer to call them.

The breeding ranges of magellanic and Peruvian penguins, *Spheniscus humboldti*, overlap in the islands of southern Chile, but they tend to breed at different times and the Peruvian species is recognized by the presence of only one stripe under the chin. The upper stripe or collar of the magellanics is absent. I have found no record of any hybrids between them. They mingle freely in the Pacific when the magellanic penguins are not breeding and tend to move northward during the winter. On the Atlantic side, where there are no other penguins along the mainland or north of the Falklands, the magellanic penguins may wander as far north as the limit of the tropics in Brazil, but they do not breed there. The Peruvian penguins have ranged and bred as far north as latitude 7°S, far into the tropics. The northern populations of blackfooted penguins also breed in the tropics, and Galápagos penguins are confined to the tropics (Map 8).

The blackfooted penguins of Africa, *Spheniscus demersus*, have a single chest stripe and are not easily distinguishable from Peruvian penguins. This is of little biological import, because blackfooted and Peruvian penguins never come into contact. There is a marked distinction between blackfooted and magellanic penguins. These two were probably of later common ancestry than the blackfooted and Peruvian penguins and they may even now occasionally encounter each other in wanderings in the Atlantic. It is noteworthy evidence of their recent separation that a small percentage of the South African penguins have a double stripe as in their magellanic cousins. That they have black feet and bray like jackasses is true of both species.

The other species of *Spheniscus*, *S. mendiculus* of the Galápagos Islands, has two stripes, including a collar as in the magellanic penguins although the width and distinctness of this is variable. Surprise has been expressed that the Galápagos penguins should differ from the Peruvians and resemble the magellanics when it is highly probable that they are more closely related to the Peruvians. However it is quite understandable that the Galápagos penguins should have evolved this distinction, or have retained it while the Peruvian penguins became distinct. The biological need, and hence the impact of selection, was just to distinguish these two, Peruvian and Galápagos, as they divided from a common ancestry, not to distinguish Galápagos and magellanics, which were not emerging from the same common ancestry and have never been in contact as developed species.

The penguins in this genus well illustrate the tendency for similar warm-blooded animals to be larger in cool and smaller

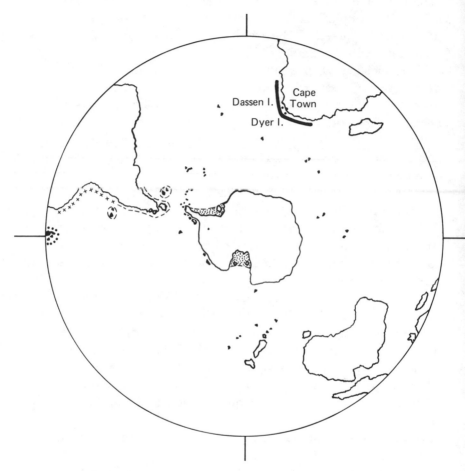

8. *Distribution of breeding colonies of* Spheniscus *penguins, indicated as on Map 5.* Dassen and Dyer Islands, not shown on the other maps, have been inserted because they have large colonies near Cape Town.

▬▬▬▬ Blackfooted (*S. demersus*)
– – – – Magellanic (*S. magellanicus*)
× × × × × Peruvian (*S. humboldti*)
o o o o Galápagos (*S. mendiculus*)

in warm environments. Magellanic penguins, which range farthest south and into coolest waters, average about 11 pounds (about 5 kilos) in weight; Peruvian penguins, overlapping but generally more northerly, about 9 pounds (about 4 kilos); blackfooted penguins, ranging up into the tropics on the west coast of Africa, about 6½ pounds (about 3 kilos); and Galápagos penguins, on the equator, only about 5 pounds (about 2¼ kilos). All build nests of quite varied materials in holes that they dig themselves if the digging is good, or they nest in nooks and crannies if it is not. All usually lay and incubate two eggs. The breeding seasons are strongly affected by the different climates, even within the range of some single species, a point for later discussion (see Chapter 6).

The birds in the genus *Eudyptes* are the crested penguins, so called because all have crests or tufts of feathers on the head. To a casual observer all look much alike, but on closer study this is evidently the most highly differentiated genus of living penguins. I have listed six species, following B. Stonehouse and a number of other students. However another of the leading students of the group, J. Warham, lists only five as distinct species and gives different names for two of them. The use of different names is a technical matter, due to some question as to exactly which species were intended by some early authors. That does not matter much as long as one is consistent, and I will be. The problem of number of species arises from the fact that these various groups have evolved relatively recently and indeed are still evolving. If two populations are tending to become distinct, it is difficult or sometimes impossible to determine whether they have passed a point of no return that commits them to continuance as genetically distinct groups. Such cases are among the most convincing and most interesting examples of evolution at the level of speciation.

The first point raised here is whether royal penguins and

macaroni penguins are still subspecies or have become distinct enough to be separate species. The answer may seem almost obvious because royal penguins in their usual form, at least, are the most easily distinguished of all the crested penguins. Their chins and the sides of their heads are white, whereas those parts are black in other crested penguins, including typical macaronis. However, occasionally a white-marked bird turns up among macaronis and a black one among royals. That could be and by some students is considered evidence that the two are still interbreeding. Nevertheless and even if that is so, which is not really established, interbreeding must be so reduced that I would consider it only hybridization between already distinct species, a phenomenon not rare in birds.

Another question is whether the fiordland and the Snares Island penguins have really passed the point of no return. They are fairly close neighbors and to my eye, at least, they look almost exactly alike. However, they breed at different times of year and there is no evidence that they interbreed, so almost all students do consider them distinct species and I must go along.

The species as here accepted and named are thus as follows, with their most evident recognition marks:

> *E. chrysolophus*, macaroni: the crests are a rich orange and originate from a broad band of that color across the forehead
>
> *E. schlegeli*, royal: crests about as in *E. chrysolophus*, but chin and side of head nearly (or quite?) always white
>
> *E. crestatus*, rockhopper: crests yellow, no forehead band, anterior end of crest well separated from bill, posterior end flopping
>
> *E. sclateri*, erect-crested: crests yellow, originating near bill, posterior end stiff and erect

    E. pachyrhynchus, fiordland: crests similar to erect-
crested penguin but not erect, skin around bill dark,
cheek often vaguely striped
    E. robustus, Snares Island: like fiordland penguin but
skin around bill paler and cheek rarely striped

Macaroni and royal penguins average about 10 pounds
(about 4½ kilos) in weight, erect-crested about 8 pounds
(about 3½ kilos), fiordland and Snares Island about 6½
pounds (about 3 kilos), and rockhopper penguins about 5½
pounds (about 2½ kilos). Here and wherever weights are
given it must be remembered that these vary greatly among
individuals and with the season. Nevertheless their averages
do indicate the relative sizes of the species. Among crested
penguins also the size varies with sex, males being larger.
That is true of most, perhaps of all penguins, although it is
better documented in the crested penguins than in some.
Also in some species the difference is so small or overlap in
range of size so great that human observers cannot readily
determine the sex of living birds. In this genus there is no
particular correlation of size with latitude.
    All the crested penguins are colonial, some rookeries with
enormous populations. The males are pugnacious, and there
is considerable threatening and downright fighting in the
crowded rookeries. They are also quite willing to attack human
observers. Except for a few macaronis on the Antarctic Peninsula all the crested penguins breed on islands, and on at least
six islands two species of this genus occur, sometimes even
within the same rookery (Map 9). Wherever two species of
Eudyptes are associated, one of them is *E. crestatus*, the rockhopper, and the other is a larger species. On Macquarie
Island rockhoppers and royals both occur and must be
fishing the same waters, but their nests are in quite different
areas of the island. Rockhoppers and *E. sclateri*, erect-crested

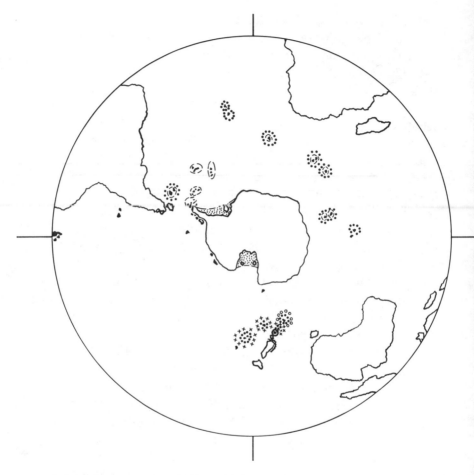

9. *Distribution of breeding colonies of* Eudyptes *penguins, indicated as on Map 5.*

penguins, are said to occur together on Campbell, Antipodes, and Bounty Islands, but I do not know how closely they are associated there. In the Falklands and some other islands rockhoppers and *E. chrysolophus*, the macaroni, occur in the same rookeries. In such cases the larger species generally lays somewhat earlier than the smaller rockhoppers.

Macaronis breed on several of the subantarctic islands and on others as far south as the South Sandwich and South Shetland Islands, a few even on the Antarctic Peninsula. They are correctly reported as breeding birds in the Falklands, but they are rare there and may be strays from South Georgia, where they are abundant. They usually occur in the Falklands only as one or a few couples scattered among the enormous rookeries of rockhoppers, the commonest Falkland penguins and the only other species of *Eudyptes* in those islands. It has been reported, but I am not quite sure how authentically, that occasionally a lone macaroni comes ashore there and in the absence of a mate of its own species breeds with a rockhopper, an extraordinary instance of hybridization in penguins if true. Those I saw in the Falklands were loyal to mates of their own species.

Rockhoppers are typically cool-temperate to, at most, subantarctic penguins (Fig. 10). They get around far and wide and occur on almost all the islands right around the world between about 30°50'S and 50°40'S. Their main range is between the Antarctic and the Subtropical Convergence, but they are north of the latter in the Falklands and on Tristan da Cunha. The other four species of *Eudyptes* are much more restricted in breeding ranges. Erect-crested penguins breed in large numbers at Bounty Island (47°43'S, east of the southern tip of New Zealand) and Antipodes Island (49°42'S, south of Bounty Island) and are said to breed in lesser numbers on Campbell Island (52°30'S) although I saw none there. Strays are also said to land rarely at the southern tip of New Zealand

and may even occasionally breed there. Royal penguins are known to breed in only a few enormous rookeries high above the shore on a single island, Macquarie, at latitude 52°30′S, although when not incubating or feeding young they navigate far at sea and occasionally land on more or less remote coasts. The other penguins on Macquarie are kings and rockhoppers, well distinguished from the royals and staying out of the royal rookery.

Fiordland penguins breed in the rain forests along the fiords of the southwestern part of South Island, New Zealand, and around to Stewart Island, south of the main south island, and smaller adjacent islands. This species, too, had a Maori name, but authorities differ as to whether it was *pokotiwha*, *tawhaki*, or *tawaki*. The last two are obviously variants of the same word. The first is most likely for this species and the second may have been a synonym or someone's mistake. It is too late to settle the matter now because there are no Maori speakers left where these penguins live. (There still are some where the *kororaas* or little blues live.)

Snares Island penguins are known only from a small group of islands less than 80 miles (about 110 kilometers) south of Stewart Island.

The individual nesting habits of the crested penguins are as varied as their greatly different environments, from rain forests to icy subantarctic islands. Most seek shelter of available kinds, but rockhoppers, true to their name, gather on open, bare, often very steep rocky slopes. As far as definitely known, all usually lay two eggs but tend to discard or somehow lose the first, sometimes as soon as the second is laid, and they usually incubate only the second egg, which is larger than the first.

I have found no really satisfactory explanation for the extraordinary difference in size of the two eggs and usual

loss of the first, smaller egg. The most nearly plausible explanations, not necessarily contradictory, are two alternatives
suggested by Warham. It is hardly possible for these birds
to rear more than one chick. Egg loss is high and may be due
largely to the aggressiveness of the males, and that is countered
by the sacrifice of one egg. The population can afford to lose
(at least) half its eggs, especially the smaller ones. Or, since
only one can be reared, it is adaptive to have two chances
to have at least one hatchling, but if two do hatch it is adaptive
for one to be behind the other so that food and energy will
not long be wasted in trying to rear both.

The typical member of the last genus as these are listed
here is *Eudyptula minor*, smallest of the living (or for that matter
of the known extinct) penguins, adults sometimes weighing
as little as about 1½ pounds (about 0.7 kilo) and averaging
only about 2⅕ pounds (about 1 kilo). (I am indebted to
Bernard Stonehouse for these and other weights of penguins,
although I have modified them slightly.) Usually called fairy
penguins in Australia, they there occur along much of the
coast from Sydney (latitude 33°55′S) on the east around Tas-
mania to the south (to 43°30′S) and up to near Fremantle
(32°07′) on the west. In New Zealand, where they are usually
called "blue" or "little blue" penguins by whites, but *kororaa*
by Maoris, they occur around the whole coast of North
Island and around both the northern and the southern ends
of South Island. Besides their small stature, they are distinguished by the almost uniform pale slaty or (to some
eyes) bluish gray head, back, and wings, with no crests or
other special marks (Fig. 11). They usually lay and incubate
two eggs and nest in solitary burrows, made by themselves or
borrowed when otherwise available, or sometimes in natural
holes and crannies.

Here there is another problem of classification because on

the South Island of New Zealand, on the Banks Peninsula and Lyttelton Harbor and the adjacent coast north and northeast from Christchurch there are closely similar but usually distinguishable penguins. These are somewhat heavier, perhaps about 3⅓ pounds (about 1½ kilos) in average weight and with a white band along the front edge of the flipper. These are commonly considered a separate species, *Eudyptula albosignata*, white-flippered penguins. However, Stonehouse, a leading authority, says that in the coastal zone between typical *albosignata* and *minor* there are intermediate penguins indicating probable interbreeding and suggesting that *albosignata* is only a local subspecies of *minor*. (I may also say that in my admittedly slight experience with *albosignata* it does not look really distinctive.) However, experienced observers from the Canterbury Museum in Christchurch assured me that the two are perfectly distinct and that they do not believe that either customary interbreeding or occasional hybridizing is occurring.

Thus we do not really know exactly how many species of living penguins there are: eighteen if *Eudyptula albosignata* is specifically different from *minor* and *Eudyptes schlegeli* from *chrysolophus*; seventeen if either one is a good species but the other is not; sixteen if neither one is. Some students would reduce the number to fifteen. Even worse, the question has been raised whether the nominal four species of *Spheniscus* might not "really" be only three, two, or one, so it could be argued that there are only twelve living "full" species of penguins in all. I believe that all four species of *Spheniscus* merit recognition, and although I have my doubts about the status of a couple of other species, I continue to list eighteen. Such cases are to be expected, and it may not even be sensible to ask exactly how many species there are. Evolution is a fact, and when two species arise from what was previously one the process is usually gradual. There is no exact time when they become "really" separate species. As a rule they just become more and more nearly separate until finally, after many generations, there is no longer any real question.

Throughout this chapter, and indeed most of this book, I have been writing in terms of the sixteen species now generally considered distinct plus the two that are sometimes considered subspecies only. Earlier stages of evolutionary differentiation can also be found among living penguins, especially those with large ranges geographically and into different environments. For example northern and southern gentoos are somewhat different and are commonly listed as two subspecies. The same is true of northern and southern little blue penguins in New Zealand. These separate populations are beginning to differentiate and there is probably little genetic interchange, by interbreeding, between them at present. If the situation remained much the same for a few hundred thousand years, which is far from likely, these present subspecies might well become different species.

Such are the penguins now gracing the earth, incomparably more varied, more colorful, more widespread, more interesting, and also more instructive than might be gathered from the stereotyped pseudo-adélies of cartoons and tales.

6. Penguins' Life Cycles

The delightful occupation of bird watching usually consists of observing the visible, sometimes also the audible, characteristics of a bird, looking up its name in a guidebook if it is new to the observer, and entering that name in a life list. Of course all watchers do know that there is more to a bird than its recognition pattern or song, and they also derive pleasure from watching a bird go about its daily activities. Carrying that still further to encompass the whole life of a species of birds requires still more single-minded devotion, available time, and mobility, for outside of tropical lowlands few birds pass their whole lives in one area. This pursuit soon becomes much more than amateurish, for it needs not only long concentration of effort but also a background of knowledge and special skill in observation.

Penguins as a group offer special difficulties but also some special advantages in those respects. A few species are relatively accessible. Fairy penguins (or little blues) come ashore nightly in large numbers near the large city of Melbourne, Australia, where they are a tourist attraction. In southern New Zealand the yellow-eyed penguins usually hide away in the tussock grass, but sometimes make nuisances of themselves by nesting near or even under houses. Most penguins, however, spend their shore time on islands, especially, or in some cases on other shores that are difficult of access, offer few or no living amenities for researchers, and tend to have what humans consider most unpleasant climates. Moreover, penguins spend much of their time at sea, often a total of half their lives and continuously for days or weeks, in some species even for months. Aerial-flying oceanic birds are not too difficult to observe at sea, but penguins are spotted there almost by accident if at all. On the other hand most of them are easily observed while courting, laying, and raising chicks.

Even now relatively little is known about the activities of penguins when they are in the medium to which they are primarily adapted. Nevertheless a great deal is known about the other activities of most species, and more is being learned every day. Continuous multinational programs for antarctic and subantarctic research include studies of the numerous penguins in those vast areas. Research on the still more numerous species, but usually less numerous individuals, of temperate-zone and tropical penguins has been more sporadic. Less is known today about the lives of magellanic penguins, first to be made known to Europeans and of relatively easy access, than about adélies, discovered centuries later and confined to antarctic regions. Study of the relatively northern species has sometimes been by more or less isolated but able and enthusiastic local ornithologists than by coordinated research campaigns. I have mentioned the outstanding study of yellow-eyed penguins in New Zealand by Richdale, and there have been similar but generally less detailed studies of several other nonantarctic species.

As long as a species continues to exist, it does so through the repeating life cycles of its members. It is not easy to decide the most logical or significant point to begin an account of those continuous cycles. For a penguin or any other bird, hatching seems analogous to birth and is a beginning, but before the hatching must be incubation. Before incubation must be laying. Before laying, if a new life is to result, must be fertilization. Before fertilization there is normally, at least, some form of preparation for what is to become a family, various among different species but often including such things as territory establishment, pair formation, and nest building. And, for migratory species, before all that must come return to the geographic area where breeding occurs.

The differing life cycles of the various species depend, although not in uniform ways, on such factors as seasonal regimes and land and oceanic environments. Adélies are migratory, have strong seasonal cycles, are stereotypic although not otherwise typical of penguins, and have become the best known. Let us start with them.

Adélies spend the Antarctic winter dispersed along the edge of the pack ice and in more or less adjacent waters. When the southern spring begins, generally in early October (corresponding to April in the northern hemisphere), they migrate to the shore, which by this time may be visible from the edge of the ice but is more likely to be tens of miles away. Each penguin goes, with few errors, to the rookery where it was born or, when it is older, where it was breeding the year before (Fig. 12). The ability of penguins to find their way home, even from far out at sea, is extraordinary. It is not thoroughly understood, and indeed the ability of birds in general to find their way, migrate, and navigate still is somewhat mysterious despite years of intense study. It is established that penguins, like some other birds, can orient by the direction of the sun and that they have some unknown kind of internal clock that compensates for daily apparent movement of the sun. That makes all the more mysterious whether and how those south of the Antarctic Circle navigate during periods when the sun does not rise.

The adélies have been feeding during the winter and most of them are now fat and in good condition, prepared for what will be a long total fast for many of them. Most of the first arrivals at the rookery are mature and comparatively heavy males. The others soon straggle in. Couples formerly mated usually arrive separately and apparently have not been spending the winter together. They tend to get together now because both, and more especially the males, have a sense of location and territory and tend to resettle where they had a nest the year before. The first comer of a pair, often the male, at once sets up a territory, starts building a nest, and goes into what are usually, but surely incorrectly, called ecstatic displays, with head pointed upward and wings spread. If last year's mate does not soon turn up, a different liaison generally results. The arrival of the previous mate thereafter may result in a violent squabble with varying outcome. Mates are fairly constant and clearly do recognize each other, but what may be anthropomorphically called the divorce and remarriage rate is considerable.

That matter of recognition becomes more vitally important later on when success in raising a chick depends on parents and offspring recognizing each other. It has already been discussed (Chapter 5) that each species as a whole has visual recognition patterns. Individuals, however, are not recognized visually. Individuals within a local specific population evidently look as much alike to penguin eyes as to human eyes. That is not true of voices. Penguin cries sound much alike to humans, but to penguins they are individually recognizable. Stonehouse has remarked that if penguins knew that we recognize each other mostly by sight they would think us foolish and abnormal. It is so much easier and more natural to recognize voices!

Breeding success in crowded adélie rookeries depends on defense of a minimal territory, large enough for a nest and small enough to defend against neighbors even while on the nest. Diameters of 2 to 2½ feet (roughly 60 to 80 centimeters) are common. All conjugal affairs and care of nestlings go on only within a territory, and individuals or couples without a territory cannot successfully mate and breed. Territories are held by constant vociferous quarreling and occasional battle.

As soon as a territory is occupied, nest building begins and it goes on continually until the chicks leave the nest. The nests are roughly circular, usually around 15 inches (about 40 centimeters) or somewhat less in diameter, and saucer-shaped, built up with pebbles or other solid bits, such as old bones, of manipulatable size. Suitable materials are usually at a premium, and one of the commonest, most constant activities in an adélie rookery is stealing pebbles from each other. An experimenter once put a supply of specially colored pebbles at one point in a colony and found them soon spread almost evenly over the whole rookery. A courting male may present a nice pebble to his chosen mate.

Copulation begins soon after a couple is established in a territory and goes on vigorously for some time, reaching a height in late October or early November. Shortly thereafter egg laying begins. Two eggs, of about the same size, are usually laid, with an interval of one to five days between them. Occasionally if one or both eggs are lost one or two more will be laid. When the eggs have been laid, the female, who has been fasting for perhaps a month, takes off for open water (now less distant) and the feeding grounds or rather waters. Although the male has been fasting about as long or probably a bit longer he stays home and incubates the eggs until the female, now well fed, comes back, which may be as much as three weeks later. By now the male has gone without eating for up to two months and may have lost as much as 40 percent of his weight. Now he finally gets a chance to feed. Thereafter the two incubate in relays with shorter periods. Incubation in all takes about a month or somewhat longer.

The hatchlings for the first ten days or so have poor temperature regulation and might freeze to death if left uncovered for even a few minutes. During this period continuously and thereafter for some time periodically, they nestle under one or the other of the parents in turn. The nestlings are finally

1. RECOGNITION MARKS OF SOME PENGUINS.

APTENODYTES

Emperor

King

EUDYPTES

Macaroni

Rockhopper

Erect-crested

Royal

Fjordland

Snares Island

MEGADYPTES

Yellow-eyed

2. RECOGNITION MARKS OF SOME PENGUINS.

Blackfooted

Magellanic

Peruvian

Galápagos

SPHENISCUS

Adélie

Chinstrap

Gentoo

PYGOSCELIS

Little Blue

White-flippered

EUDYPTULA

3.   Gentoo penguins with one king penguin and a seal on Macquarie Island.

4.   A busy adélie penguin and a pile of elephant seals in the South Shetlands.

5.   Blackfooted penguins in their nooks in South Africa.

6.   Galápagos penguins on the rocky coast of Isabela Island, Galápagos.

7. A mated couple of macaroni penguins among rockhoppers on New Island, Falklands.

8. A royal penguin on Macquarie Island.

9. A yellow-eyed penguin in the tussock grass near Dunedin, New Zealand.

10. A pair of rockhopper penguins on Macquarie Island.

too large for two to fit altogether under one parent and the sight of the big babies with their heads or rears sticking out from under mama or papa is ludicrous to human eyes (Fig. 13). During this time the parent not on nest duty goes out to sea, open water being close by now, and comes back with food, mostly bright red krill (small crustaceans, euphausiids) which are regurgitated into the babies' mouths, or taken by them out of the parent's mouth.

For the first two weeks or so after hatching, the chicks are covered with lustrous light-gray down. This is then replaced by the second down, which is coarser, duller, and brown in color. They are becoming increasingly active and shortly leave the nest and gather with others of their age in what could be called a kindergarten but is usually called by the French word *crèche* which originally meant crib or manger but now means also day nursery. (The adélies were, after all, named for a French woman.) At this stage the chicks are still in down which would become waterlogged if they entered the sea. Therefore, although practicing a sort of adolescent independence from the nest, they are still completely dependent on their parents for food. Their growing appetites give the parents a full-time job to feed a maximum of two chicks. No penguins can successfully raise more than two, and some species can raise only one.

Early observers thought that the crèches were in fact functionally nurseries, but that is not the case. The young in a crèche are not guarded and there is no communal care and no feeding other than by parents. The crèches are nevertheless adaptive in several ways. They cut down predation because skuas, the principal predators on the young, for reasons not obvious rarely attack the young in a crèche although they may quickly attack one that strays away. In cold weather the young huddling together in the crèche also help to keep each other warm.

The big babies in a crèche shriek for food, and they chase any adult penguin that comes up from the landing place and hence is presumed to be loaded with food. In spite of this violent importunity—we have seen adults knocked right back into the sea by the onrush—parents will feed only their own chicks (Figs. 14, 15). After all, they do have almost more than they can manage without giving handouts (beakouts?) to the neighbors' kids as well. Here recognition by voice becomes a necessary adaptation for specific survival. If parents did not tend assiduously to their own offspring, many of the young would have no chance. The larger, older, or more aggressive young would get all the food.

If a bad storm should strike after the young have left the nests and are in crèches, they crouch and huddle even more tightly together, forming what the French call a *tortue* or tortoise. They are thus less likely to be completely snowed in and, still more, they keep each other warm, giving a better chance of surviving the Antarctic weather, which is unreliable even in summer.

Then, after about another month, as the brief summer is drawing to a close, the chicks shed their second down and in ten days or so acquire full but immature plumage, which differs from adult plumage most obviously in their having a white, rather than black, chin (Fig. 17). Now the young can start swimming and can feed themselves. They are fully emancipated from their parents or, perhaps more significantly, the parents are emancipated from them. The parents are free from nests, territories, and young, but now they molt, often out on the ice although during the period of molt they cannot swim and must again fast. Finally with new waterproof feather suits they settle into winter quarters again around the edges of the pack ice at variable times but generally in March. Some, at least, of the young have usually preceded them, and there seems to be no bond between parents and young after emancipation.

The young molt again and acquire adult plumage in their second year, but they do not breed before the third year. The average beginning of breeding is not until the fifth year and a few males do not breed until the eighth year. I have not found a firm figure as to how much longer they may live. The early, inexperienced breeders, especially those in their third and fourth years, often make mistakes, suggesting that instinct at first is not enough. Maturity is also needed, and probably some sort of learning. The inexperienced may not be successful in mating, may make nests at the wrong time, may fail to take proper care of eggs and young, or may do other things that are from a Jovian (or evolutionary) point of view serious blunders.

Even the experienced breeders on an average fall far short of raising chicks from both eggs. An egg that rolls out of the nest is not retrieved. Skuas and a few other birds get many eggs and young chicks. Even a few minutes' delay in changing the guard may result in death to egg or hatched offspring. An unusually heavy snowfall may imprison a whole colony and kill many of the birds. Parasites and diseases exist, but may be less prevalent than in warmer climes. Survivorship varies greatly and data on it are not extensive, but it appears that it may be usual for only one-quarter of the eggs laid to be represented by living chicks toward the end of the summer in which they hatched. Data on survivorship of old birds are even more scanty, indeed almost nonexistent, but it would seem that most of them die at sea, perhaps especially by onslaught of leopard seals, their principal predators. In spite of the hazards of their lives, the adélie populations, and those of most penguins, are holding their own and even increasing, a subject to which I will return in Chapter 8.

I shall not go into the life cycles of other species in nearly so much detail, partly because that would involve more than most people want to know about the subject and partly because it would require more than anyone does know. Even though the adélies are unique in their summer breeding in the farthest south, some features of their lives are much the same as in other penguins and it will suffice to point out main differences, when known.

Next we may consider the emperors, which breed in extreme latitudes, as far south but not so far north as the adélies. They have a completely different seasonal rhythm. The emperors spend the summer at sea and on sea ice. The dates of their activities vary from place to place and time to time so that there are apparent discrepancies depending on where and when observations were made. (That is equally or even more true for the adélies.) For emperors the best data are probably those collected over twelve winters at the French station near Pointe Géologie in Adélie Land, although that colony, almost on the Antarctic Circle, is farther north than many emperor rookeries. There the emperors arrive over a period of about a month, mostly in March (equivalent to northern September) and start to take off again when the ice breaks up, usually starting around mid-December (equivalent to northern June). Sexual activity reaches its height around late April and early May, eggs are laid throughout much of May, are incubated for about two months, and so mostly hatch in July (northern January).

The emperors sometimes come ashore and occasionally breed there, but usually they stay and breed on shelf ice or fast ice along the coasts. They are the only penguins, indeed the only birds, that can and often do spend their whole lives without ever coming on land. Like the adélies and all the antarctic and subantarctic penguins the emperors live in crowded rookeries or colonies. They have a similarly stylized courtship, but they do not make nests or defend territories. There is accordingly more peaceful interaction in populations or social groups. In bad weather, which may be virtually continuous, not only the young in crèches but also the adults form *tortues*.

Once they start toward the land-fast ice, the emperors do not eat again until they return to the open sea, and for the males this may mean that they are totally without food for some three months. As soon as an egg is laid, the male takes it onto his feet and tucks a fold of warm flesh, usually ambiguously called a pouch, over it. There it stays for the two months or a bit more of incubation. The females take off to sea and food for those months, coming back with some food in store to regurgitate for the young at about the time when hatching occurs. The males then have a chance to feed and thereafter the pair take turns feeding their offspring. As soon as the weather and their strength permit, the still downy young congregate in crèches apart from their parents, who must continue to feed them. At this stage the chicks have a strange appearance, unlike that of any other young penguins. The down of the head is dark, but a large white circle surrounds each eye and between the circles a white band runs under the chin (see Fig. 1). It has been surmised that this helps the parents to locate chicks in Antarctic darkness. As with adélies and indeed all penguins, the emperors recognize their own chicks and are unwilling to feed others.

By the time the near-shore ice breaks up, which may vary from late December to February in various places and years, most of the young must have replaced their down with normal penguin feathers and be able to swim and to feed themselves, although some may complete the molt on floe ice. Chicks hatched late in the season are likely not to make it and to perish. The peculiar way of incubating the egg and protecting the very young chicks makes it impossible to hatch or raise more than one each year. Figures on survivorship vary greatly and are not plentiful, but it appears that the emperors are capable of maintaining and even increasing their populations under what are undoubtedly the most extremely adverse breeding conditions of any birds on earth. The system of close parental care and of weathering storms in *tortues* is highly effective. Data gathered some fifty years ago on captive emperor penguins (in zoos) indicated the astonishing average longevity of over 34 years. There are few reliable data on longevity in penguins in the wild, but it is probable that few emperors and no other penguins ever reach such a great age. Penguins are nevertheless unusually long-lived as birds go.

As previously noted the somewhat smaller king penguins resemble the emperors and are closely related to them (Fig. 18). Nevertheless they breed under very different circumstances and their annual cycles, also unique among penguins as are those of the emperors, are completely different from the emperors. They breed on islands north of the pack ice and in the cool-temperate to, broadly speaking, subantarctic zones. Like the emperors they normally lay a single egg and incubate it and for a time shelter the hatchlings on their feet and under an abdominal fold. Like the emperors, also, they therefore build no nests and have no territories, but the resemblance does not go much further. They breed on land, on muddy flats or sodden fields of bunch grass (tussock), the footing becoming a foul slime oddly at variance with the usually markedly well-kempt birds.

After a period of courtship, kings may lay their eggs almost any time from November to March but with two fairly well-marked climaxes, one early, perhaps in December, and another late, more or less in February. Incubation, although not quite as long as for the emperors, does last nearly eight weeks. Thus the southern summer is well along for hatchlings from eggs laid in December (corresponding to northern June) and is effectively over for those from eggs laid in February (northern August). All the year's hatchlings winter over at the colony and are fed at long intervals, about every three to four weeks, by their parents. The infant down is drab and uniform, quite unlike the strange baby garb of emperors. The spring after they were hatched the young molt into juvenile but waterproof plumage and can go off to sea for food and generally fend for themselves. Their emancipated parents molt, court, and start over again with a new egg.

The extraordinary thing about that cycle is that it occurs in strongly seasonal climates and yet is not synchronized with the year. The time from one egg to the next for any given breeder is fourteen to sixteen months. Thus an early breeder one year could be a late breeder the next year but could not again breed successfully in the third year. It is usually said that a couple can produce a maximum of two offspring in three years. Since, however, there is little successful egg laying from April to September, it seems to me (although I must not quarrel with the adept students of these birds) that perhaps a pair with a regular cycle of sixteen months might just barely produce at most one chick in half the years (two years on, two off). The cycles apparently do not go like clockwork. King penguins do not breed until they are several years old and, as with all penguins, inexperienced breeders have poor success, frequently abandoning their eggs.

Even were the facts all known, which is far from being the case, there would remain many questions about the lives of the beautiful kings, unique among penguins as penguins are unique among birds. Why do they lay a single egg and incubate it on their feet when they live in climatic zones where all other penguins have nests and many incubate two eggs? A conjectural answer would be that the common ancestor of kings and emperors was adapted to breeding in colder, more stormy climates where incubating and brooding on the feet and under an abdominal fold gave the chick maximum chance of pulling through the winter. Then this habit, fixed genetically, persisted in the kings even after it was not necessarily optimal. But that only moves the question back; it does not give an answer. Why do the emperors, and by this hypothesis the ancestral *Aptenodytes*, breed in winter along the most frigid and tempestuous coasts on earth when all other seasonal penguins, including those in the same regions as the emperors, breed in summer? And the emperors, although they have a long incubation, have a comparatively short dependent chickhood so that the total breeding cycle covers less than a year. Why then do the kings, if still in some respects genetically adapted to environments like those of the emperors and no longer occupied by kings, take well over a year for one breeding cycle? That is unique among penguins but very rare among any other birds. Some other birds do breed in only half of their adult years but, as far as I can learn, their cycle from courtship to fully emancipated offspring still is not longer than a year when it does occur. It has been repeatedly suggested that as large birds require more time to develop, the exceptionally long cycle of the kings is an adaptive meeting of that necessity. But if the kings developed at rates proportional to those of the larger emperors, the breeding cycle would not necessarily impinge much if any on the three deep winter months. Their ancestors were apparently adapted to even colder climates than they now undergo. Why would natural selection have reduced their breeding capacity by lengthening the cycle beyond a year when retention of even moderately greater cold tolerance would have retained or enhanced the productivity of young?

Thus is illustrated the fact that after observations are made and organized, layer after layer of deeper enquiries and problems arise. What functions do observed activities and characteristics have in the lives of organisms? How do they relate to communities, environments, ecology? How—even more profoundly—how and why did they arise in the long history of the species?

Chinstrap and gentoo penguins, the other two species of *Pygoscelis* in addition to the adélies, have much the same life patterns as the adélies in the far south. They sometimes nest among the adélies, but in their own rookeries they tend not to be so crowded (Fig. 19). Gentoos range farther north than the others, on some islands well beyond the pack ice and in milder, but still subantarctic, climates (Fig. 20). The longer summers do not require such rigid limits on breeding dates. Among gentoos especially, dates vary considerably with localities and climates. In what is for them the far north, some of them lay in September but in South Georgia they lay late in October and in Antarctica often not until November. Where these three species occur together, competition may be alleviated to some extent by difference in size, gentoos being larger, although chinstraps and adélies are close to the same size. The ability of birds so similar in food, habits, and habitats to live in great numbers in the same areas should have more study than has yet been devoted to it. Observers have commented on their differences in temperament: gentoos rather timid, adélies more indifferent although capable of fits of anger, chinstraps exceptionally pugnacious.

The crested penguins, species of the genus *Eudyptes*, have life cycles similar in many ways but modified by their wide range in latitude and habitats. All are colonial and highly social, usually living in large crowded rookeries (Fig. 21), although this is less true of the fiordland and Snares Island penguins, and a few rockhoppers do live in small groups. These are long-lived birds and they rarely breed until their fifth year, often not until the seventh to ninth. Once started, they breed annually. As noted in the last chapter, they lay two eggs of unequal size but usually only the chick from the second, larger egg is hatched, let alone raised. It may be added, however, that the smaller egg is viable and that both may hatch, probably most commonly in the fiordland penguins. Still it is an effort, often an impossible effort, to feed two chicks, and the smaller of the two usually dies before being fledged.

As in adélies and indeed colonial penguins in general, crested penguins tend to retain the same mates and the same nesting spots from year to year. All crested penguins spend about half the year at sea throughout their adult lives, but the times of the year spent at sea vary with the weather, the climate, and the species. The whole breeding season lasts only 18 to 21 weeks. The males usually arrive at the colony site a week or so before the females, and as much as a month may be spent in fighting, displaying, nest building from whatever is available (usually pebbles or twigs), and finally laying. Male and female take turns incubating and eating, the latter at sea of course. Incubation takes about five weeks. While the hatchlings are still in the nest, a matter of three or four weeks, the males stay ashore, fasting, and protect them from cold or in general stand guard duty. During this period the females bring food to the young (but not to their mates). Thereafter the young form crèches and both parents are free to gather food at sea, although the female is likely still to do most of the feeding. As in adélies, and in all penguins, the parents now recognize their own young and will feed no others. Finally when ten or eleven weeks old the young are fully fledged and can go to sea at about the same time as their parents, although now not in family groups.

Having completed their domestic duties for the year, the adults stay at sea for one or two months fattening up. Then they return to their colony sites to molt and refledge. That may take as much as a month, during which time they cannot swim

and must again fast. Finally they go to sea again, now for
about four to six months, during which they may travel
great distances, although most of their life in the open ocean
remains mysterious.

The cycle is about the same for all crested penguins, but it
may begin at quite diverse times. Among fiordland penguins,
in a comparatively equable climate, it begins in winter, often
fairly early in July (corresponding with northern January),
but on the subantarctic islands it usually begins in September
or October (equivalent to March or April). Correspondingly,
fiordland chicks may go to sea in November, others not until
January or February. When two species of crested penguins
breed on the same island, a fairly frequent occurrence, the
larger species starts breeding first by as much as a month.
For the several years before they, too, breed, the young
return to their birthplaces each year, arriving after the breeding adults and just hanging around making nuisances of
themselves. Prebreeding or otherwise unoccupied penguins
of various species are sometimes called hoodlums, an an-
thropomorphism that does strike me as apt.

Although penguins of the genus *Spheniscus* were the first
seen by Europeans, are extremely numerous, and have been
encountered by hundreds of scientists and tens of thousands
of other humans, scientific studies of these have not been so
extensive as for the more southern species. Anecdotal men-
tions are numerous; the early ones are usually accounts of
killing them for food, the later ones more likely to be mere
mention of seeing them. There are some scientific accounts for
all four species. One of the most nearly complete was recently
published by two authors (Boswall and MacIver) on the
basis of observations at Punta Tombo, on the east coast of Patagonia, made while taking a film for the British Broadcasting
Company. There is a colony, or metropolis, of magellanic
penguins over a million in number in that small area, and it

has become a major tourist attraction without inspiring anything like the concerted scientific studies of antarctic and subantarctic species. The South African species has received attention as much for its supposed damage to fisheries as for any other reason.

The magellanics are the most southern species of *Spheniscus* but breed in cool-temperate rather than subantarctic areas. The Peruvian and blackfooted (or African) penguins are subtropical to tropical and the Galápagos penguins are exclusively tropical. Where they are numerous, the *Spheniscus* penguins live in large crowded colonies as at Punta Tombo, but smaller groups may spread out and become almost solitary (in couples) and the Galápagos penguins are not numerous at any single locality. All like to nest under shelter (Fig. 22), under shrubs or even within their roots where available, in burrows where shrubs are not numerous enough and the ground is soft enough for digging, in nooks and crannies where necessary as in the lava flows of the Galápagos. I have seen blackfooted penguins nesting under a castaway sheet of corrugated iron.

The relatively southern magellanic penguins (see Fig. 9) spend approximately April through August at sea and more or less September through March at and near their breeding grounds. They are largely migratory and move north (on rare occasions even as far as the tropics) in the southern winter, although in the Falkland Islands a few may be seen about even in winter. Stonehouse has shown that the migration tends to keep them in water of nearly the same temperature throughout the year. Within their burrows or other shelters they make a sketchy nest of vegetation or anything else portable that is lying around, and they lay two eggs of equal size. Both eggs are incubated, mostly but not exclusively by the female parent, for about six weeks. The hatchlings go through two downs, first gray then brown, more or less like the adélies and some other penguins. They do not form crèches but are fed near their shelters by their parents. Finally they are fledged about 75 days after hatching. The juvenile plumage is dark except for the white abdomen and fronts of legs and, oddly enough, white patches on the cheeks where adults have black patches. I have found no reliable data on longevity or on time of full maturity, except that the latter is later than the second year.

Peruvian and blackfooted penguins, closely related to the magellanic, are similar to the latter in most respects. These penguins are often kept in zoos and there is a record life-span of at least eighteen years for a blackfooted penguin in a zoo. Average span in the wild is certainly shorter.

A detailed study of Galápagos penguins has been made by Dee Boersma but as I write this only a study of thermoregulation in a few captive individuals has been published. There are now only between 11,000 and 25,000 individuals, making this the least populous species of penguins with the possible exception of the white-flippered penguins. They breed only on the western islands Fernandina (Narborough to the English) and Isabella (Albemarle) (Fig. 9). Breeding is determined largely by surface water temperature when it locally falls below about 75° F (24° C). That occurs at unpredictable intervals when the cool and rich waters of the Cromwell Current upwell around these islands. Then the penguins molt, and almost uniquely among penguins the molt is a prelude to breeding. These penguins also differ from almost all others and indeed from most other birds in that they may breed more than once a year and may breed at any time of year, distinctions correlated with their equatorial habitat. Two eggs are usually laid, and they hatch in succession not both at once. Of the chicks, two, one, or none may be successfully reared, depending mainly on the food supply. The parents usually spend night on shore and their cruising range is quite limited.

I have already mentioned that the life cycle in the yellow-

eyed penguin is unusually well known thanks to some eighteen
years of careful observation by Richdale. Here that extensive
knowledge will be only briefly summarized. These penguins
are less colonial than most of the more southern species and
live in small scattered groups in near-shore areas of bunch
grass (tussock) or scrub. Neighbors do interact and there is
even some mate swapping, although many who change mates
are widows or widowers. Some two-fifths of the marriages
("pair bonds" is the more sober term) last from two to six
years, and a few, about 3 percent, last from seven to thirteen
years.

These inhabitants of a region with equable climates do
not migrate and, next to those of the Galápagos, are among
the most sedentary penguins. They stay near their breeding
grounds the year around and rarely stay at sea as long as a
week at a time. Nevertheless their breeding is sharply seasonal,
two eggs being laid in late September to early October and
then incubated for about six weeks. The chicks are fed for
fifteen or sixteen weeks, until middle or late March, after
which the adults undergo their annual molt. Some breed in
their second year, but with little success. More mature adults
of four years and later have excellent success in hatching
eggs, some 80 percent, but mortality in the first year is high.
The full potential life span is not exactly established, but some
individuals known to be over twenty years old were still
vigorous and breeding.

Finally the two doubtfully distinct species of *Eudyptula*, the
little blues or fairies and the white-flippers, are the smallest
of all known penguins, living or extinct, and are unique in
some other ways. All other penguins are almost strictly diurnal
when on their breeding grounds. Their behavior at sea is
not well known, but from reports of sailors hearing them bray
at night it appears that magellanic penguins may be partly
nocturnal away from land. The little blues, on the contrary,

are highly nocturnal, seldom seen out of their shelters during the day. That and the habit of nesting and in general secreting themselves in burrows or any available hole or nook may be related to heavy predation by day. (Recently the worst diurnal predators are men and dogs, but that can hardly be the historical origin of the penguins' secretiveness.) Although the little blues may be fairly numerous and even locally crowded in some favorable breeding areas, they are less social or colonial than most penguins. In some places in Australia considerable numbers, into the hundreds, do tend to go to sea and to return together in a sort of daily parade that has become a tourist sight. In other places in Australia and, as far as I have seen, in New Zealand, each bird or family is effectively solitary.

These penguins live in comparatively mild and equable climates and the breeding is less clearly seasonal than for most penguins. Some breeding goes on throughout the year, but it tends to be more concentrated in the spring. For the most part a single clutch of two eggs is laid, but there are a few records of a couple's breeding twice in one year. Thereafter the sequence is little different from that of various other penguins. Male and female usually alternate in incubation and in feeding the young. Hatchlings have a gray first and a brown second down. After their offspring are fledged and emancipated, the parents molt and then go off to sea. They are nonmigratory but may travel for considerable distances between spells of breeding duty.

7. More Behavior and Some Ecology

There is something irresistibly human about an adélie penguin hurrying along an antarctic beach, upright, preoccupied, progressing with quick short steps as if late for an appointment. It is easy to think of many penguin activities in human terms. They fight with their neighbors; steal from each other; quarrel with their wives but also give them gifts of rare stones; divide chores between mates, sometimes quite unevenly; often take good care of the kids but sometimes neglect or even kill them; are frequently true, in their fashion, to mates, but sometimes have affairs and often are, in effect, divorced and remarried; play games; shout; make messes—the list could be prolonged. Anyone who has spent much time penguin watching must be convinced that penguins are conscious, that they think, and that they have emotions. More extensive and analytical observation, however, results in conviction that their thoughts, their emotions, and probably even the quality of their consciousness are not like ours.

A common comparison is that birds as a class act more instinctively than humans. Psychologists and ethologists are not altogether happy with the concept or definition of "instinct," and much human behavior is less consciously thoughtful than we might like to think. Yet it is certainly true that penguin behavior is incomparably less varied, more by rote, and in some degree more often unlearned than human behavior. That is also true of other birds, some of which appear to have larger repertories than penguins, although that may mean only that they have been more intensively studied. Even anatomically the nervous systems of birds are so unlike ours that different behaviors and different mental lives are inherent. Penguins are literally, as well as figuratively, bird-brained.

The most obvious distinctions of a bird brain are the simplicity of the cerebral hemispheres, with slight development of the cortex, which is associated with what we consider higher mental functions in mammals, and the enormous development of a basal part (corpus striatum) of the forebrain, supposed to be associated with more stereotyped behavior. (There may be a bit of circular reasoning there.) Birds have a poorly developed sense of smell, and although I know of no good technical study of this sense in penguins it may be even less developed than usual in them: many of them have reduced external nares (nostrils) or may even lack these, breathing only through the mouth. The sense of hearing, usually good in birds, is certainly excellent in penguins, who are sensitive to such subtle variations in the calls of other penguins.

Some penguins, notably those of the genus *Spheniscus*, are among the very few vertebrate animals that have no binocular vision whatever. That is, the fields of vision of the two eyes are completely different, with no overlap—a great peculiarity for us who have almost entirely binocular vision. I first realized this on meeting a blackfooted penguin (*Spheniscus demersus*, you recall) in South Africa who couldn't believe what he (or perhaps she) saw with one eye and so continually turned the head from side to side to scrutinize me with one eye after the other. Since then I have seen the same thing done by other penguins and have learned that it is duly recorded in the literature of animal behavior. Other penguins, such as the adélies, do have slight binocular vision used especially for distant view, but they are likely to use one eye after another for closer study. I have found no report on color vision in penguins, but practically all diurnal birds have good color vision and there is no reason to doubt that they have too. That seems so normal to us that we tend to take it for granted, but in fact many animals have poor or no color vision. The fact that the only distinct colors on penguins themselves are between yellow and orange does hint that their spectral range might be somehow limited.

Some aspects, perhaps the most important aspects, of penguin behavior were covered in the preceding chapter and a few others earlier in this book. Those need not be carried further but they do suggest a few remarks bearing on questions of instinct. It was noted in passing for some species that when they first begin to breed they are quite poor at it, and indeed that seems to be usual among penguins. Inexperienced breeders lose most of their eggs or young through sheer ineptitude. Only after they have been at it for a few years are they able to raise viable chicks from most of the eggs they lay. That certainly suggests that good parenthood is learned rather than instinctive, or that the instinct requires maturing before it really takes hold, or, most likely, some of both. Since no penguins raise more than two offspring at most in a breeding season and many only one, that would seem to put them at a disadvantage in maintaining population numbers. But penguins are long-lived and one penguin may have twenty or more breeding cycles so that failures in the first few need not lessen the population or even prevent a population explosion under favorable conditions. Other apparent failures of instinct are that penguins will happily incubate rocks or other objects of suitable size in place of eggs and that emperor penguins are so eager to adopt stray chicks that rival foster parents may literally tear a chick to pieces. Those, however, are examples of adaptive instincts, or at least impulses, rather than failures of them. Substitutes for eggs are rare and a fervor for incubation tends to preserve real eggs. Strays are in grave danger in the emperors' environment if there is no tendency to adopt them.

Persistent penguin watchers acquire many anecdotal impressions of penguin temperaments. Although some, notably rockhoppers and chinstraps, may attack if approached too closely and too suddenly, penguins tend to be imperturbable and are often called tame, although that word has inappropriate connotations. They like company and even the few noncolonial species are given to socializing with others of their kind, and also in some circumstances with others not of their kind, such as penguins of other species or humans. Penguins acquainted with humans seem to accept us as only another quaint and somewhat clumsy kind of penguin, just as we tend to think of penguins as quaint and somewhat clumsy humans.

Although penguins are so well adapted for aquatic life and spend such a large part of their lives at sea, they act as if they felt safer on land. If frightened in the water near shore, they will usually make a panicky landing, but if frightened on land they will usually waddle or toboggan away without heading for the water. That must be related to the fact that for adult penguins the most dangerous predators are marine. Penguins sometimes establish rookeries at considerable heights and thus put themselves to what seems to us the useless labor of scrambling up and down steep paths. One observer (R. H. Beck) has said that some gentoos on small islands have their rookery right across the island on the other side from their landing beach. Years ago, when I thought it possible that I could do a little penguin mind reading, I suggested that such behavior might result from their wanting to get as far from the sea as possible. Now I do not know.

In this connection I should mention another attempt at penguin mind reading (not by me) that has had wide circulation but is almost certainly wrong. When a mob of penguins is going to sea, they will often mill about on shore for some time before taking the plunge. The story is that they finally chuck one of their number in, then watch to see whether this test victim survives before the rest of them follow. It might happen that one is accidentally pushed in by the pressure of the crowd behind, but there is no evidence of intention. Usually the first in is just a bit more eager, active, or decisive. That is how he happened to be ahead to begin with. In groups of penguins, whether on land or in the sea, anyone who takes off in a seemingly purposeful way is likely to be followed slavishly by his gregarious fellows.

Many mammals, especially young mammals, behave in ways that can be interpreted only as playful. That is not characteristic of birds, and young penguins, even after leaving the nest, do not do anything much more interesting than chasing about screaming for food or just standing with (one feels) empty minds. There is, however, an eyewitness account of adult adélies hopping onto a passing ice floe, taking a ride, then hopping off and running back to repeat the performance on the next floe that came along. If humans did that, they would be playing. I don't know what, if anything, the adélies thought they were doing.

Study of bird behavior that is more than anecdotal was stimulated and channeled if not originated by Julian Huxley's studies of the great crested grebe, first published in 1914. Activities of the grebes were analyzed into a number of units, each a sort of stereotype that was programmed into a sequence. These included, for instance, the "search" or "Dundreary" attitude, the "cat" display, or, especially interesting here, the "ghostly penguin" attitude and the "penguin dance." In the "ghostly penguin" a courting bird bobs up vertically from the water, wings at side and head bowed, and in the "penguin dance" the mates bob up simultaneously, swim toward each other, and face with bits of water weed in their beaks. The ethologists, a school of students of animal, especially bird, behavior, have ever since followed and refined that approach of unit analysis with such interpretive concepts as the "ritualization" of behavior and "displacement" when an activity functional in origin takes its place in a "ritual" where its original function is no longer relevant.

Penguins do not in fact assume Huxley's ghostly penguin attitude or perform his penguin dance, but their behavior is to some extent "ritualized" in Huxley's sense and it does lend itself to the same sort of unit analysis. I have already mentioned the so-called "ecstatic" attitude, one of the first such units to be abstracted and (misleadingly) named. More recently such studies of penguin behavior have been greatly expanded in extent and detail, although they can be considered nearly complete for few species. Not surprisingly, the adélies have been most thoroughly ethologized, most recently by E. B. Spurr and by D. G. Ainley from two different points of view. J. Warham has done much the same for crested penguins (the genus *Eudyptes*) with the added refinement of sonograms (pictorial frequency analyses) of many of their calls. (All three reports are in the book edited by Stonehouse, listed at the end of this volume.)

Without discussing the sonograms in detail, it may be said that they do show individual differences among penguins of the same species. Thus there is a concretely established basis for individual recognition among penguins by calls that to human ears seem indistinguishable. The sonograms show more marked differences among different species, and in fact human observers well familiarized with penguins can often recognize species by their calls.

Warham has analyzed the crested penguin displays and vocalization in terms of their functions as communications. In abbreviated paraphrase his categories and examples of each are as follows.

1. Avoidance of conflict and lessening of aggressiveness.

    The slender walk: head lowered and flippers thrust stiffly forward. Used on entering a colony.

    Allo-preening: simultaneous preening by two birds, each of the other's head and neck. Sometimes with chicks, but usually reduction of tension between adult male and female.

2. Resistance against aggression and prevention of trespass on territory.

    Threat displays: when intense, neck outstretched, head bobbed up and down, mouth agape, hoarse cries and growls uttered. May be followed by contact fighting.

3. Recognition.

    Bowing: usually by breeding pairs, bill pointed down into or toward nest and deep, throbbing cries uttered.

    Calling: the usual penguin recogniton signal, as between parent and chick.

    Trumpeting: bowing, thrusting head forward, and shouting. Usual when a bird joins its mate after a long absence.

4. Signing off.

    Head shake: end of message.

5. Maintenance of pair bond and recognition of mate.

    Bowing: as above.

    Mutual display: male vertical head swings (see 6) and female on nest reaches toward him and calls.

    Mutual trumpeting: mates trumpeting together. When intense, mutual vertical trumpeting occurs, with heads raised and pointed upward.

6. Advertising ownership of nest territory.

Vertical head swinging: head bowed, then head
and flippers raised, head swung from side to
side and finally vertical, with series of braying
cries. Usually by males.

These birds also have a "stare around" posture, a "sub-
missive" posture, a wing "shiver," a "flipper flick," a "quiver-
ing" display, a "shoulders-hunched" posture, and of course a
coition posture, as well as such miscellaneous and unritualized
(not Warham's word) activities as head shaking, yawning,
scratching, and self-preening.

For the ádelie penguin Spurr has made what must be a
definitely exhaustive analysis from the simplest "elementary
acts" to fairly elaborate "displays" of various sorts. His list
follows, with brief explanations of terms not self-explanatory.

Rest (standing or lying).
Comfort activities: preening, stretching, yawning, scratch-
ing, and shaking.
Walking: ordinary or "slender," the latter the same as
Warham's "slender walk" among crested penguins.
Looking around.
Nest building, divided into a sequence of five activities.
Copulation, including a premounting "arms act" with
the male vibrating his flippers.
Incubation.
Withdrawn crouch: an attacked penguin flattens down
and keeps still.
Attack, with various methods, a sort of penguin judo.
Chase.
Escape.
Threat displays. Six are recognized and named. The
number has been increased by analytical splitting of
what other students have considered single displays.

These are:

Bill-to-axilla: beak tucked into one arm (flipper) pit.

Sideways stare, either lying down or standing up.

Alternate stare: looking first with one eye and then the other.

Point (with beak), either standing or lying.

Gape, a sort of point with beak open, also either standing or lying.

Charge, bill closed or bill open (but "charge!" without a saber).

Sexual displays. Four of these are distinguished:

Ecstatic, a standard penguin performance, head up, wings flapping, voice building up to a loud noise. It is commonly given by courting males, but sets off others in the vicinity. Oddly enough, the approach of a human can set it off. Who do they think we are? This display must have been observed long before, but it was first fully described and named (misnamed) in 1907 by Edward A. Wilson, a great ornithologist and bird artist who lost his life in 1912 returning from the South Pole with Scott.

Bowing, just what it sounds like.

Loud mutual display, also what it sounds like, except that it is not always mutual; a lone penguin may also pose and scream. It can be done with bill forward or raised.

Quiet mutual display, done with bill raised, head waved, and a low growl.

Spurr goes on to a statistical analysis of how often and in what circumstances each named display or sequence of displays was observed. He derived a flow chart for courting and coition which merits presentation (in somewhat different form and with facultative omissions and without repetitions):

Male: ecstatic——→sideways stare→bow→stand in nest——→
Female: approach→sideways stare→bow→stand near nest→

Male: lie in nest→work on nest→stand near nest→
Female: (away) ————————————→stand in nest——→

Male: (away) ————————————→arms act——→
Female: lie in nest→work on nest→still in nest→

Male: mount—————————→
Female: raise head & tail→

Male: copulate
Female: copulate

Similar but in general much less detailed analyses have been made for some other species, but further details need not be given here. I will only mention that such displays as the ecstatic, although so widespread in penguins, do not occur in emperors or in species that nest in burrows.

I have no wish, intention, or competence to criticize such studies. They are painstaking, enlightening in many ways, and always interesting. Just because they are so interesting, I do think about their significance. Is it possible that the recognition of a fixed number of named "displays" is an artifact of classification rather than a fact about penguins? Obviously no male penguin thinks, "Now I've gone through 'ecstatic' and 'sideways stare' and I'm getting on with this cutie, so I'll go into my 'bow,' " and no ethologist has or would think of the matter in that way. Yet I sense some feeling that a minimum unit of behavior is not just a convenience of description but may have validity as a unit of instinct or learning, a building block from which more complex behavioral events and sequences are constructed. Many of us would boggle at the idea of analyzing our own behavior in the same way, and this would require at least a much longer list both of "elementary acts" and of "displays," but it could be done. I am uncertain whether that implies a weakness in our study of human behavior or in that of penguin behavior.

Another broad aspect of behavior must be briefly mentioned. That is that behavior is a major factor in adaptations to environment and in ecological roles. Much of this again is evident in what I have already said. It can be exemplified by the fact that adaptations to weather, climate, and the movement between land and sea are not only physiological, as has been mentioned, but also behavioral. Once penguins have passed their first few days out of the shell their heat production, insulation, and thermoregulation are so effective that they are likely to have more trouble keeping cool than keeping warm. That is particularly evident in the many penguins that live in comparatively warm climates—in the temperate zone and the tropics. They all have behavioral traits that differ from those of antarctic and subantarctic penguins and help them to keep cool. Most of them nest and breed in burrows or other retreats away from the sun. The one or two species of *Eudyptula* are largely nocturnal. Species like the Galápagos penguins that spend some time on land away from their retreats stand in the shade, hold out their wings to expose the radiating undersides to the air, and pant rapidly when the air temperature rises.

Much about the general ecology of penguins is also evident from preceding chapters and a special aspect, interaction with man, will be treated in the next chapter. A few other remarks are to be made here.

Penguins seem to have little effect on their own environments. In the big rookeries they void enormous amounts of excrement. Approaching such a rookery from afar, one smells it first, hears it next, and sees it last. Any potential fertilizing effect is usually made inconspicuous by the trampling of so many flat-footed birds. Presumably large amounts of excrement are voided at sea as well, and that may be recycled in a way through marine plants and then onward into animals, including penguins again along the way. In spite of their great numbers and voracious appetites, penguins have not evidently upset the balance of nature at all unless man has become involved somewhere in a cycle, a subject for later consideration.

The penguins' own places in food chains are quite well established. The food chains that involve them start with floating marine plants (phytoplankton). Those are producers, using the energy of light and the materials in sea water to synthesize food. They are mainly diatoms but algae and some other photosynthetic organisms also enter into the picture. Next come small, floating or feebly swimming, plant-eating animals (herbivorous zooplankton), mostly krill (euphausiids) in the Antarctic, other crustaceans, varied invertebrates, and some fishes elsewhere. These are primary consumers.

Penguins may feed directly on krill, thus coming in as the third link in a food chain, but they may feed on fish which have fed on primary consumers, thus putting the penguins in the fourth place up the chain, or on squid which fed on fish which fed on primary consumers, putting penguins in fifth place. Thus penguins can occur at the third, fourth, or fifth trophic level, which is the technical expression for separate links in a food chain, starting with primary producers as the first trophic level. Although I have not used many technical terms in this book, "trophic" is a useful one for anyone interested in ecology to know. It comes from a Greek word meaning nourishing and is not to be confused with "tropic," which means turning. (The Tropic of Cancer and Tropic of Capricorn are where the sun stops its apparent movement north or south, turns about, and goes the other way.)

Not the last trophic level but the sixth and last to be dealt with here consists of animals that eat penguins, from their eggs to their old age, either as carrion or as prey. There are many different animals at this level, depending on factors such as latitude, area, and season. In the antarctic and sub-antarctic regions, skuas (relatives of gulls) are the principal predators on penguins on land but sheathbills and giant petrels also take eggs and occasional chicks. Sheathbills manage to get much of the food being regurgitated for penguin chicks and to transfer it to their own chicks, which is not predation but is an unusual trophic interaction. In southern waters leopard seals are persistent aquatic predators on penguins. Killer whales are not likely to bother with penguins of average size but do prey on emperors to a limited extent.

Farther north the land predators on penguins include a number of other birds, especially among gulls, eagles, and hawks; and in Africa, ibises, as well as foxes and, in Australia at least, also snakes and large lizards. In the Galápagos, land crabs have been known to attack penguin chicks. In comparatively warm waters seals are still important predators on

Table 3.   Trophic Relationships of Penguins

*Food chains**   *Trophic levels*

penguin predators
(skuas, seals, etc.)   6

                                    penguins   5

            penguins   squid   4

penguins   fish   3

            primary consumers   2
            (krill, etc.)

            primary producers   1
            (diatoms, etc.)

*Arrows point from what is eaten to what eats it.

penguins, but in these more northern areas usually fur seals and sea lions. Sharks certainly and probably other fairly large predaceous fish are also involved. In some anticipation of the topic of the next chapter it may be mentioned that animals introduced by man, intentionally or not, have also become predators on penguins, including dogs (even in the Antarctic) and rats among others.

In spite of their numbers, it appears that none of those predators is fully dependent on penguins for food. All can and do eat other food and for most of them a penguin or its egg is a welcome snack but not a regular meal. Skuas are probably most involved with penguins and they often nest near penguin rookeries. If the penguin crop were poor or lacking, the number of skuas would doubtless be somewhat reduced but they would still get along.

Table 3 gives an idea of the trophic relationships of penguins but it is oversimplified. The full trophic picture for any community would be an intricate web rather than so simple a set of a few connected chains.

8. Penguins and Man

Penguins and men were undoubtedly interacting long before Europeans discovered penguins. It is known that natives of Tierra del Fuego hunted penguins both for their meat and for their skins. The Maoris of New Zealand ate many birds— moas, takahes, kiwis, wekas, tuis, and others—which along with rats, mussels, and some fishes were rare sources of protein. All went by the name of *huahua*, a word that (contrary to another book on penguins) did not signify young birds preserved in fat. It is reasonable to suppose that Maoris also ate penguins, especially after they had killed off all the moas, but I have found no definite evidence to that effect. It also seems probable that some African natives ate penguins or their eggs, but again there seems to be no clear evidence. Penguins were still very abundant in all those regions when they were explored by Europeans so it is unlikely that native predation had much effect.

It was indicated in Chapter 1 that it was a sad day for penguins when Europeans did encounter them. Another account adds to the evidence, which is all too clear. This was written by Richard Hawkins in 1594 (quoted by Crawshay in 1907):

> The flesh of these Pengwins is much of the savour of a certaine Fowle taken in the Ilands of Lundey and Silley, which we call Puffins . . . We salted some doozen or sixteene Hogsheads, which serued vs (whilest they lasted) insteed of powdred Beefe. The hunting of them (as wee may well terme it) was a great recreation to my company and worth the sight. . . . In getting them once

within the Ring close together, few escaped ... and
ordinarily there was no drove which yeelded vs not a
thosand, and more: the manner of killing them which the
Hunters vsed, beeing in a cluster together, was with their
cudgels to knocke them on the head.

A small anecdote demonstrates that the views of Hawkins'
crew on recreation are still current. Not long ago I was
arranging a boat trip in Lyttelton Harbour, the port of
Christchurch, New Zealand, in search of white-flippered
penguins. I was asked not to tell anyone the locations of any
nests we might find, for if they became known the birds would
certainly be killed. The early explorers at least had the excuse
that they needed food.

I have not tried it, but by all accounts penguin meat is not
epicurean and was extensively used only as an adjunct to
ship's stores even less tasty or as alternative to no meat at all.
On the other hand all accounts indicate that fresh penguin
eggs range from acceptable to delicious. The gathering of
them has continued right down to our own day and has
resulted in practically wiping out some populations of penguins, at least temporarily and locally. In the Falkland Islands,
until recently, November 9th was traditionally devoted to
egg-hunting and was a holiday for the schoolchildren. The
date (somewhat flexible) was of course chosen as one when
penguin eggs would have been laid but would still be fresh.
It was also chosen to coincide with the English Lord Mayor's
Day, for reasons that I can't imagine. Egg gathering was, and
is, by no means confined to the single day. Colonies near
Port Stanley, the only town in the Falklands, were wiped out,
but eggs were brought in by the tens of thousands in boats from
more distant rookeries. The messes created when the fragile
eggs were simply dumped into open holds hardly bear think-
ing about. One also wonders how, or whether, so many eggs

really were consumed, as Port Stanley even today is hardly more than a village.

Most of the eggs so exploited were from rockhoppers, which were and still are much the most numerous penguins in those islands. Magellanic nests were also robbed, but less freely as those birds nest in burrows and egg robbing is more difficult. It is also said that eggers came back from magellanic colonies heavily infested with fleas. The situation regarding king penguins is not clear. It has been supposed that those birds were originally abundant in the Falklands but were for a time completely wiped out. There is even a story, possibly false, that the last king penguins were exterminated by a shepherd, not by egg robbing but by boiling down the birds for oil to put on his roof. However that may be, most of the early records (from about the middle of the 18th century) suggest that the king penguins were always rare in the Falklands. There may have been none breeding there early in the present century. At present there are a few, not enough to merit designation as a rookery at any point.

Penguin eggs are still being gathered in the Falklands, but on a smaller scale. In some places the magellanics are even protected and encouraged by sheep farmers there because they fertilize the bunch grass ("tussock" or in the Falklands commonly "tussac" and sometimes "penguin grass"). There are also a number of bird sanctuaries established under a Native Reserve Ordinance and including some penguin colonies. Apart from the kings, penguins still are very abundant in the Falklands, especially in some of the outlying and remote western islands. Fairly recent estimates put the number of rockhoppers as "approaching five millions," magellanics also in the milions, and gentoos about 200,000. Macaronis have apparently always been and still are present, mostly in rockhopper colonies, but rare.

Blackfooted penguins breed in great numbers on islands

near Cape Town, and there, too, egging was formerly done on a large scale. In the 1890s the yield from one small island (Dassen) alone was said to be about 300,000 eggs each year. Gangs of men went through the colony every day during the laying season, scooping up every egg with receptacles on the ends of long sticks. It is hard to understand how the colonies survived such treatment, but they did, only to encounter a new menace to be mentioned shortly.

In addition to loss of their eggs, penguins suffered enormous assaults on their persons during much of the 19th century and well into the 20th. Their skins were used for articles of clothing, from shoes to caps, as well as floor mats and even, noncommercially, for roofing. The most extensive slaughter, however, was for oil obtained by rendering out the thick layer of fat that all penguins have before undergoing the fasting ordeal of the breeding season. Thus was supplemented the oil obtained from whales and seals, especially elephant seals, in the latitudes where penguins are common. The penguins are so much smaller that it took thousands to equal the oil yield of one large whale, but the penguins were always vastly more numerous than whales and incomparably easier to catch and kill. One source in the 1860s indicates that it took eight penguins to produce one gallon of oil, but it is not clear what species of penguins was involved. Apparently one of moderate size.

The most notorious incident occurred in the 1890s and into the first part of the 20th century when one Joseph Hatch was given a concession by the New Zealand government to kill penguins for oil on Macquarie Island. After giving up on the king penguins, he fell to on the royals and cropped about 150,000 per year. Taken when fat, just as they came in before the breeding season, these are said to have averaged about a pint of oil per bird, which again is about eight birds per gallon. After more than a quarter century of that there was so much public outcry that in 1919 the government withdrew the concession and Hatch went out of business in spite of his claim that the royals were even more numerous than when he started. In fact he was probably right. He was taking only a small fraction of the population, and the remaining breeding pairs were quite capable at least of replacing the loss. The island is now a sanctuary and has no inhabitants except for scientific investigators.

Egg gathering and penguin hunting on a commercial scale have now ceased, and their continuance on some small scale is not a serious menace. Rockhopper penguins, for example, have long played an essential part in human life on the extremely remote island group of Tristan da Cunha in the South Atlantic, and they still do. Eggs are eaten, some oil is rendered for home use, moulted feathers are stuffed into mattresses, and skins are used to make mats and hats as well as various small objects, some for sale as souvenirs. But humans are extremely few and penguins extremely many at Tristan da Cunha.

Penguins are now protected almost everywhere and gathering their eggs, if not entirely banned, is sufficiently controlled. Penguin eggs were being served in restaurants in Punta Arenas, on the Strait of Magellan, as recently as the 1960s, but that has been stopped and Chile is protecting penguins. Nevertheless, human activities have been unfavorable to penguins in several other ways and continue to be so. For one thing, humans have introduced many new predators into regions occupied by breeding penguins. Everywhere, including the Antarctic, these include dogs. In many places they include rats, which eat penguin eggs and sometimes chicks. In New Zealand there were no mammalian land predators until men introduced not only dogs and rats but also cats, stoats, and ferrets. In the Galápagos there was one native mammalian land predator, a rat, but man has introduced others more dangerous: dogs, cats, and Norway rats. It must be granted, however, that in no case are introduced predators known to have caused an appreciable reduction in total penguin populations. A probably unique case is that on Tristan da Cunha one entire rookery of rockhoppers was wiped out by hogs, but there are still immense rookeries of that species in that island group.

Off the west coast of South America and the west and south coasts of Africa penguins of the genus *Spheniscus* lived on bird islands where they occupied burrows in the deep deposits of guano, formed in part by the penguins themselves but in larger part by flying oceanic birds. In both areas the guano has been shipped away to be used as fertilizer. Thus in many instances the homes of the penguins have been literally dug up and removed. That has definitely had an adverse effect on the penguins, although again they have managed to survive it in large numbers.

The encroachment of civilization is rarely good for wildlife, and it is not good for penguins, but it has not yet affected them very widely or deeply. Most penguins breed in remote, scantily or not populated places. Where they do nest near cities, as in the vicinities of Melbourne, Australia, Dunedin, New Zealand, or Punta Arenas, Chile, they do sometimes seem a bit harassed, but they are still getting along. There have been arguments and complaints about possible effects of increasing tourist travel to the Subantarctic and Antarctic, and perhaps there is a future danger, but so far I cannot see any serious ill effects. Tourists are not numerous and they come and go quickly—there are no land accommodations whatever for them in those regions. They love the penguins and do not aim to harm them or even to disturb them unduly. In fact I believe that the scientists studying penguins, although obviously I approve their efforts, do far more to disturb the birds than tourists do. Moreover in Antarctica, explorers, supporting personnel, and nonbiological scientific personnel do not have clean records in their relationships with penguins, which they have often upset, robbed, or killed for food, for trophies, or for fun. Yet all this has had little effect on the southern penguins as yet.

There is another human activity not directly connected with penguins at all that seems to have the most ominous possibilities for those birds: oil spills. While the Suez Canal was closed all oil tankers bound westward from the oil fields of the Near East had to go around the very dangerous waters off South Africa. The supertankers or "very large crude carriers" (VLCCS), increasing in number, must continue to do so. There have been repeated wrecks and large spills there, especially near the islands Dassen northwest and Dyer southeast of Cape Town. Both those islands have large breeding colonies of blackfooted penguins and large numbers of them have been oiled in slicks from the spills of wrecked tankers, as well as from oil deliberately jettisoned from tankers.

In the usual course of things, an oiled penguin dies. Heroic efforts have been made by the South African National Foundation for the Conservation of Coastal Birds (SANCCOB), in Cape Town, to bring in oiled penguins from Dassen and Dyer. Then they are carefully cleaned and hand-fed until they can again care for themselves and be returned to the wild. Many die despite tender loving care by SANCCOB (Fig. 23). The total number killed cannot be counted or even reasonably estimated. Many die at sea and never get back to the home island, while others continue to die long after a spill. It has been said that the numbers of that species have been reduced from "millions" to "an estimated forty thousand," but that is a guess and not necessarily a good one. All that can reasonably be said is that a significant percentage of those populations has been killed. More are sure to die in the future.

Not long since—on 9 August 1974 to be exact—that menace

moved in on another species of *Spheniscus*. On the night of that day the Shell VLCC *Metula* went aground on a shoal in the Strait of Magellan and spilled about 16.8 million gallons of Arabian crude oil, the second largest spill ever. (The largest was the *Torrey Canyon* off the Scilly Isles, also killing many seabirds but at least no penguins.) That occurred less than 40 miles (about 60 kilometers) from the Isla Magdalena, one of the "Penguin Islands" of early voyages. Many magellanic penguins were killed. No one knows how many except that it must have been many more than the "2500 to 3000" finally admitted reluctantly by a naturalist commissioned by Shell and the oil industry.

It has been a rather sad story up to this point, as stories of man's contacts with wildlife are all too likely to be. At least it can be said that no species of penguin has become extinct through the activities of man, a negative sort of triumph especially as some activities seem almost to have been calculated to lead to their extinction. The blackfooted penguins are in some danger, and that danger is likely to increase and may spread to some other species. The population of white-flippered penguins (a doubtfully distinct species, you recall) is small and they may be in danger because their limited area is near large human populations. The Galápagos population is also small and living in a limited area but less frequented as yet. There is no evidence of immediate danger for any other species.

Haven't we humans been at all helpful to the penguin populations in a positive way? Well, yes we have, but in a way that is ironic. We have slaughtered the big southern whales and brought some of them to, if not indeed beyond, the threshold of extinction. This slaughter, now shamefully exclusive to the Japanese and the Russians, has depleted the cetacean consumers of krill. That has left more food available for krill-eating penguins, notably the adélies and the chinstraps. There is good evidence that those species have, in fact, increased in numbers as whales have decreased. It has been estimated that whaling activities release enough krill to feed from 200 to 300 million more penguins each year—amazing figures but vouched for by good authorities (W. B. Emison and W. J. L. Sladen).

Offhand you might say that penguins have done no harm to men worse than giving some of us a nip or two when we annoyed them, but you could run into an argument on that. Penguins eat seafood. So do men, and sometimes the same kinds. Specifically the *Spheniscus* penguins off the west coast of South America and the southwest of Africa eat enormous numbers of small fish, anchovy-like, that are also pursued by human fishers. I mentioned that the blackfooted penguins seem to have been studied from this point of view as much as from any other. One such study estimated that there were 103,000 blackfooted penguins on the islands off the southwest cape region in Africa and that their food was 94 percent fish, 5 percent squid, and 1 percent crustaceans. It was further estimated that in one breeding season they ate about 7,000 tons of food and that of this, 2,900 tons had economic value for humans. The fisheries are not crazy about penguins, but the oil spills will probably save them from the penguin menace.

Finally, the question may be asked, "What good are penguins?" It may be crass to ask what good a wild animal is, but I do think the question may also be legitimate. That depends on what you mean by good. If you mean "good to eat," you are perhaps being stupid. If you mean "good to hunt," you are surely being vicious. If you mean "good as it is good in itself to be a living creature enjoying life," you are not being crass, stupid, or vicious. I agree with you and I am your brother as well as the penguin's.

There are other legitimate and reasonable answers. One

is even a materialistic answer. Penguins are part of a complex ecology. They fit into the trophic web and they constantly renew the fertility of the seas in which they move so skillfully. They help to maintain the existing balance of nature. If they did not exist, the balance would be different. If they were removed, the balance would be upset.

Penguins are beautiful, interesting, inspiring, and funny. They are a pleasure to watch even though they do smell and their voices are not melodious. Some of them even breed in zoos, an indication that some, at least, are able to adapt well to life in captivity. They are extremely popular exhibits in zoos and oceanariums, many of which go to great effort and expense to obtain and keep them. This is viewed with some ambivalence by bird lovers or particularly by penguin lovers. Those in charge of such exhibits are usually shy about giving facts on mortality, preferring to give maximum survivals (often not impressive) rather than death rates. The scanty data available do clearly indicate that the great majority of the thousands of penguins that have been captured for shipment to zoos and the like have died either in transit or in the first few weeks at their destination. The mortality is especially high for the antarctic and subantarctic species, most desirable as exhibits but hardest to acclimatize in European, American, and Japanese zoos. It is commonly argued that zoos are justified as means of breeding animals and preventing their extinction, but this argument does not apply to penguins. Few of them do breed in captivity, and when they do the young commonly die before themselves reaching breeding age. And in fact most of the species, especially those in the far south, are breeding and maintaining populations quite successfully in the wild.

On the other hand, the captures for exhibition are not at present endangering any species, and living penguins are delightful as exhibits and are viewed with great pleasure and empathy. They are thus seen and enjoyed by millions of people who will never see them in the wild. We must decide whether this outweighs and justifies the too early deaths of hundreds of penguins.

Penguins regale us further as images in cartoons, printed and animated. They are familiar as puppets and as dolls. They are also familiar as trademarks, including one for a whole library of books. They inspire some of us to travel far to see bones of their ancient relatives, to watch their living selves, and to come home and eventually write books about them.

Some Other Publications About Penguins

There are dozens of books and hundreds of articles about penguins. These are some I like best or have found most useful, or both. They are all for adults and include no fiction, but they range in level from simplest popularization to highly technical. Brief comments will help each reader to make his own selection.

HOLDGATE, M. W., editor. 1970. *Antarctic Ecology*. Academic Press, London and New York. (A thorough symposium on the subject; Part IX, "Ecology of Antarctic Birds," has interesting chapters on or including penguins by Carick and Ingham, Stonehouse, Young, and Sladen and Leresche.)

JARVIS, C., editor. 1967. Penguins in Captivity. *International Zoo Yearbook*, vol. 7, section 1. The Zoological Society of London. A short professional symposium on the problems of keeping penguins in zoos.

KEARTON, C. 1930. *The Island of Penguins*. Longmans, London. (A personal narrative of several months spent among South African blackfooted penguins.)

LEVICK, G. M. 1914. *Antarctic Penguins*. Heinemann, London. (A general account by an early scientific authority on adélies.)

MIGOT, A. 1955. *La Faune des Iles Kerguelen et de l'Antarctique*. Connaissance du Monde, Paris. (The text of this popular book is in French, but for those who do not easily read French most of the book consists of photographs of penguins and their associates, with English captions.)

MULLER-SCHWARZE, D. 1971. Behavior of Antarctic Penguins and Seals. In L. O. Quam, editor, *Research in the Antarctic*, American Association for the Advancement of Science, Washington, pp. 259–76. (A readable summary; the other papers in this volume also give useful background information.)

MURPHY, R. C. 1946. *Oceanic Birds of South America*, 2 vols. The American Museum of Natural History, New York. (An exhaustive,

143

authoritative but highly readable account, with extended discussion of the penguins of South America and more or less adjacent islands in volume 1, pp. 329–471.)

PETTINGILL, E. R. 1960. *Penguin Summer*. Cassell, London. (An interesting, readable personal account of a summer spent studying penguins in the Falkland Islands.)

PHILIP, M. 1971. *Gregory Jackass Penguin*. David Philip, Cape Town. (An unpretentious popular account, centered on heroic efforts to save endangered African penguins.)

PREVOST, J., and J. SAPIN-JALOUSTRE. 1965. Ecologie des Manchots Antarctiques. In J. Van Mieghem, P. Van Oye, and J. Schell, editors, *Biogeography and Ecology in Antarctica*, Junk, The Hague, pp. 551–648. (Technical and in French, but with English summary and picture captions; indispensable for a serious study of penguins; this volume includes much other information on the Antarctic environment and life, although the chapter "Antarctic Birds" by Voous curiously omits penguins.)

RICHDALE, L. E. 1957. *A Population Study of Penguins*. Clarendon Press, Oxford. (A classic study mainly of the yellow-eyed penguins of New Zealand.)

ROBERTS, B., editor. 1967. *Edward Wilson's Birds of the Antarctic*. Blandford Press, London. (A sumptuous volume with a brief life of Wilson, excerpts from his journals, and many reproductions of his drawings and paintings of penguins and other Antarctic birds.)

SIMPSON, G. G. 1946. *Fossil Penguins*. Bulletin of the American Museum of Natural History, vol. 87, pp. 1–100. (My initiation to the subject; technical.)

SIMPSON, G. G. 1975. Fossil Penguins. In Stonehouse, 1975. Ch. 2, pp. 19–41. (I have not separately cited other chapters in this book, but I cite this one because it contains references to most of my other publications on penguins.)

SPARKS, J., and T. SOPER. 1967. *Penguins*. David and Charles, Newton Abbot (England). (A thorough journalistic account, interestingly and well written, marred by a few errors.)

STONEHOUSE, B. 1967. The General Biology and Thermal Balances of Penguins. *Advances in Ecological Research*, vol. 4, pp. 131–96. (A basic technical paper.)

STONEHOUSE, B. 1968. *Penguins.* Golden Press, New York. (A delightful and authoritative short popular book.)

STONEHOUSE, B., editor. 1975. *The Biology of Penguins.* Macmillan, London. (Recent work and reviews on various special aspects of research on penguins; technical but readily comprehensible for the most part; 21 chapters by 27 authors.)

STRANGE, I. J. 1972. *The Falkland Islands.* Stackpole Books, Harrisburg. (This general book on the little-known islands includes mention of interaction of men and penguins there.)

THORNTON, J. 1971. *Darwin's Islands. A Natural History of the Galápagos.* Natural History Press, Garden City. (Little about the penguins, but a thorough, popularized account of the situation in which the unique Galápagos species lives.)

WATSON, G. E. 1975. *Birds of the Antarctic and Sub-Antarctic.* American Geophysical Union, Washington. (On pages 63–83 there are good accounts of the seven most southern species of penguins.)

Index